Tibet's True Heart

Woeser

Tibet's True Heart

Selected Poems

Translated by A. E. Clark

Ragged Banner Press
Dobbs Ferry

Printed in the United States of America on alkaline paper

Cover photo: Punchstock
Author photo supplied by Woeser

The drawing of a windhorse which appears on the last page of
this book is reproduced, with permission, from the archives of
the Buddha Dharma Education Association of Tullera, Australia:
http://www.Buddhanet.net

Library of Congress Control Number: 2008926971

ISBN-13: 978-0-9816989-0-8

Ragged Banner Press
http://www.RaggedBanner.com

Postal address:
PMB 119
923 Saw Mill River Road
Ardsley, NY 10502
USA

CONTENTS

PREFACE

They were bulky, those old Party newspapers of which her father had unaccountably saved a stack. Their pages felt as stiff as the exhortations and triumphant statistics that filled them. But the little girl was intrigued, and her fingers toyed with the paper until she made an astonishing discovery: there was something under the surface. With the aid of a moist cloth, she peeled back the newsprint to find a glossy magazine page with old photos of movie stars from Shanghai. The words were difficult: some of the characters had too many strokes° and didn't make sense to her. But these images of romance and mystery were like nothing she had seen on the dirt roads of Tawu County. She spent hours meticulously peeling away newsprint to savor the beauty that had been concealed underneath. Her parents only smiled. Mao was still alive, but the Cultural Revolution had ebbed; it was no longer dangerous to own these copies of *Popular Cinema.*°

This is one of the earliest memories of the Tibetan writer named Woeser. A still earlier one is more vague. In the first years after she was born in Lhasa, her family employed a Tibetan nanny and spoke the Tibetan language at home. Life changed when she was four years old: the People's Liberation Army transferred her father, a high-ranking officer, to the east. Although they moved into what was nominally a Tibetan Autonomous Prefecture, it was part of Sichuan, and they found themselves more within the Chinese cultural sphere than before. The family stopped speaking Tibetan at home. The girl who had been called Öser became Wei Se.° Of what had gone before, all she remembered was a plane ride and a descent through the clouds that had made her ears hurt. Lhasa was forgotten.

Or perhaps not. As a college student in Chengdu, Woeser was admitted to a Chinese literature program for minority nationalities.° Segregation in the classroom made her feel more

Tibetan. This young woman of mixed ancestry (her father was half ethnic Chinese°), who had lived almost entirely in Chinese-speaking circles° and enjoyed the privileges of the daughter of a senior army commander, now began to grapple with the question of her own identity. After two years as a journalist in Dartsedo (Kangding), she seized a chance to move back to Lhasa, where she worked as an editor for the leading Tibetan literary magazine. At this time she read with shock a classified translation of John Avedon's account of the Chinese conquest of Tibet. It contradicted everything she had ever been taught. She questioned her father and an uncle who had served in the army during those years, and they conceded the foreign account was mostly correct. "[That book] had a huge impact on me," she would later tell a reporter.° "We had been taught that the old Tibet was dark and backward and a very frightening place, and that the PLA came and gave us a better life." Exploring a culture which had been not merely denigrated but largely destroyed, she found herself attracted to Buddhism, of which she had known virtually nothing in childhood but which touched a chord after her father's death in 1991.

As a writer in Lhasa who was already building a literary reputation and published a substantial book of poetry in 1999, she began discreetly to document the effects of religious repression, massive immigration of Chinese, and unbalanced economic development. She paid a price. In 2004, after her book *Notes on Tibet* was banned, she was informed that all her working hours for the foreseeable future would be devoted to her political reeducation. She sacrificed her career and moved to Beijing, where she married Wang Lixiong, an author and expert on Tibet. Though none can be distributed in China, she has had five books published in Taiwan (including a new edition of *Notes on Tibet*) and one in Hong Kong. She writes prolifically for the Internet. When the government ordered her blog taken offline in 2006, she transferred it to an overseas server. Inside the PRC, her work is accessible only to those able to circumvent the infrastructure of censorship that swaddles all digital communications. Yet she is by no means unknown. The official narrative has long represented Tibetans as good at singing and dancing and content with an increased supply of consumer goods. In comparison, Woeser's account is more humane and interesting and, as the statesman quipped, it has the added advantage of being true. Her testimony has taken on new significance in the wake of the upheaval of March 2008, whose full repercussions are not yet known.°

The girl from Tawu County is still peeling back the surface of accepted words to find something luminous or dark, but always real. Citizens of open societies could easily underestimate this achievement. In the last fifteen years the State considerably relaxed its grip on the daily life of people elsewhere in the PRC, but in Tibet these changes came late if they came at all. Visiting Lhasa in 1999, Patrick French discovered by chance that every resident of the old center of town had recently been required to sign a 'conduct agreement.'

> *There were rules on gatekeepers, rules on how to report your neighbour, rules on how much you should be earning, rules on contraception, rules on hygiene and rules on who could visit you and when [. . .] The place was ruled not by terror, as it had once been, but by constant mental supervision.*
> (French 11)

Poems such as "Showers of 1990" and "Roaming the Infinite Night" testify to the difficulty of breaking through this mental supervision. It is fortunate that Woeser succeeded. She has a distinctive voice—by turns chatty, lyrical, or wry—as she speaks of a faith under siege, the shadow of the past, and the seasons of a woman's heart.

This volume contains translations of forty-two of her poems, spanning twenty years. I worked from the manuscript of a larger collection, *xueyude bai* (雪域的白), which is being published in Taiwan. The notes which start on p. 85 seek to bridge the cultural distance that will confront the English-speaking reader; they include explanations which the poet graciously provided in response to inquiries. The ° symbol unobtrusively marks in the text those phrases and passages that are explained in the Translator's Notes, which can then be consulted, or not, as the reader chooses. A Geographical Note starting on p. 127 includes maps that indicate the places mentioned in the text.

In one of her verses, Woeser compares a poet's words to gleaming golden coins. That's a bold claim in today's China, where the valuation of poetry has declined while that of gold, in all its forms, has soared. You, gentle reader, will make your own appraisal. I hope the poems rendered here will still ring true, though in a different accent, and keep some luster under Western skies.

A. E. Clark
March 25, 2008
Dobbs Ferry

ACKNOWLEDGMENTS

Two highly literate Chinese, F. and A., labored long to help me understand these poems. Wherever in this book the tone of an idiom has been rightly grasped or a classical allusion duly noted, it is thanks to them; for I myself had only a rudimentary knowledge of the language. I regret that both have asked to remain anonymous.

Madame Woeser herself was patient and forthright in explaining some of the personal or local references in her work. I am grateful for her encouragement.

Kristina Dy-Liacco and her colleagues at the Latse Contemporary Tibetan Cultural Library answered hundreds of questions about the geography, language, and religion of Tibet. No query was too obscure or too trivial for them. The Latse Library is one of the hidden jewels of New York City.

Like Ms. Dy-Liacco, Stacy Mosher read a draft and offered helpful comments. Ms. Mosher gave me my start at translation when she was editor of *China Rights Forum*, where two of these poems first appeared with her assistance in a slightly different form. Jin Zhong, editor of Hong Kong's *Open* magazine, helped interpret some difficult phrases.

Robert Barnett generously gave the text a close reading and offered much good advice. He mentioned pertinent history, explained cultural background, and suggested many improvements of diction and phrasing.

Yangdon Dhondup supplied a pre-publication copy of her essay on Tibetan poetry in Chinese and answered questions. Lauran Hartley commented on a draft and allowed me to consult some rare periodicals at Columbia University's C.V. Starr East Asian Library. John Powers, of Australian National University, responded graciously to a question about the legacy of Padmasambhava. A long-time friend of the Tibetan people whom I will call K. had the idea for this project and suggested it to me.

While I am deeply indebted to all these people, opinions expressed in the notes should not be imputed to them. For errors and infelicities in the translation, responsibility is mine alone.

A. E. C.

Tibet's True Heart
Selected Poems of Woeser

Pray hearken to this song with five parables and six meanings,
The song with rhythm, the song like a golden string.

MILAREPA°

Remembering a Battered Buddha

Twenty days since I left Lhasa
But still I see that statue of the Buddha with its face bashed in.
It was on a street vendor's stand in front of the Tromsikhang
    neighborhood office.
I noticed it from a distance.
I'd gone to Tromsikhang Market to buy *droma*,°
But at the sight a sudden grief assailed me.
I drew closer—couldn't help it—to this thing so crushed:
It seemed alive, leaning against a shelf in agony,
The face hammered, an arm hacked off, the whole figure chopped
    off at the waist.
Hurting so bad, leaning against a rack of the goods
That surrounded it: soy sauce, bean jam, salad dressing, and roll
    after roll of toilet paper,
All introduced into our life long ago from inland China.
Around its neck an ornament, once exquisite, inlaid with colored
    stones,
And at its chest a wondrous beast with lion head and body of man,
Stacked on a fragmentary *chorten*.°
In what sacred shrine or pious home were these things once
    venerated?
Hurting so bad and leaning against the rack of merchandise,
It emanated the calm of still waters, but pain stabbed into my
    marrow:
As I looked on in grief, I sensed a story being played out
That had both a present and a past.
I was moved by the shadowy fate that had brought us together,
As if melted snow from the high peaks had filled my being.
Hugging his knees, the peddler made a pitch:
"Come on, buy it! Don't the old buddha look grand?"
"When did it get beat up like this?" I asked.

"Cultural Revolution, obviously!" he glanced up, "Had to be the
     Cultural Revolution." °
"How much?" I wanted to buy it, to take it home,
But this peddler from Jiangxi wouldn't budge from
     three thousand.°
So with reluctance and regret, and many an afterthought,
I left that broken buddha streaming rays of pain.
I only took some pictures,
So when I miss it I can turn on my computer and have a look.
Friends say it may have been a brand-new buddha, wrecked thus
To fetch a higher price, and the link to the Cultural Revolution
     was a fiction.
Maybe so; but the hurt remains.
I wrote these lines to try to let it go.

May 14, 2007
Beijing

One Kind of Emotion

Let me murmur the immemorial vow
As I gently bow my head.
A tenderness like water
Flows beneath this evening's liquid moonlight.
How should I visualize that place, so distant?
I hear a child's voice lifted in benediction.
The stars impart an icy solace.
The stationery's pale;
A couple of ordinary words stagger my heart.
I call Heaven and Earth to witness:
Life is but a cloud, a leaf.

1988
Chengdu

Let Me Write a Poem

Let me write a poem.
Let me write a poem as I'd fall in love.
But first let me leave home
With a pen in my hand and your voice in my ears,°
Impervious to others' love,
With careful tread,
Saving myself for you, pure as jade.
Let me find all kinds of paper:
Coarse for the beginning, fine for the end,
Like linen: clean and supple as can be,
Dried in the sun, and rustling in the breeze.
I'll gather all my children in,
Children older than me,
Children the man in the street bumps into every day.
Each has a particular talent:
They saunter into my mind like conceited urchins.
Absorbed in weighty duties, they make no sound.
My task? To put them down on paper at the proper time.
If one is sad, let it weep;
If one is merry, let it laugh . . .
Oh, to hear you say:
'Tis you, this mortal woman, who are my sweetheart now!

Let me write a poem.
Let me write a poem as I'd mumble in my sleep.
Then let me take it easy
Like a noble lady from another time,
Ensconced in a corner, batting my eyes on cue,
Looking lovely from a distance, though actually plain—
The kind that debauches herself at the first opportunity.
Let me struggle to make clear what weighs upon my mind.

I'll watch you draw near till you're a step away:
My ear will open sooner than my heart
To hear which phrase, which word of every day,
May prove a sturdy bridge to span the gulf.
Yet words wake me but halfway,
My other half's in torpor like the herbs in a wine bottle,°
With no one to take them out and no one to drink it down,
    or try the cure:
That's why I write a load of rubbish.
If only I could pour out my troubles to somebody!
If a word is close, let it ring out;
If it doesn't fit, let it be forgotten.
Hey, I am this mortal woman!
Can I write such a poem?

1991
Lhasa

On the Road°

On the road with edgy mind,
I'll flee the chaos of this floating world,
Pick a place to settle,
Find choice words
To tell this passing turn of the Wheel.

On the road one meets by chance
Men and women of immense dignity;
One's natural pride is humbled.
The ruins that overspread Tibet with shadows dark as night
Have a nobility not found in ordinary men.

Among those encounters:
One dear to me, long-lost,
Brilliant, uncompromising,
Neglected.
I, too, am pure and honest;
Mine, too, a sincere and gentle heart;
I wish as seasons change I could change with them.
No need for gifts to one another;
We are the gifts.

On the road, an elder of my people says:
"Golden flowers bloomed on golden mountain;
While golden flowers bloomed, he did not come;
And when he came, the flowers had died.
Silver flowers bloomed on silver mountain;
While silver flowers bloomed, he did not come;
And when he came, the flowers had died."

On the road, walking alone.
An old book without a map,
A pen, not much to eat,
Ballads from a foreign land:
These will suffice. On the road,
I see a black horse
Who does not bow his head to graze but shakes his hooves,
Vexed that he can't run free.
Yet also, deep in meditation caves among the vast mountains,
The hidden forms of men.
What sort of heart will honor and revere them?

On the road, a pious mudra's not complex,
But it ill suits a tainted brow.
A string of special mantras is not hard,
But they're jarring, from lips stained with lies.

On the road,
I clutch a flower not of this world,
Hurrying before it dies, searching in all directions,
That I may present it to an old man in a deep red robe.
A wish-fulfilling jewel,°
A wisp of a smile:
These bind the generations tight.

May 1995
Lhasa

A Midsummer Night's Dream

Many mosquitoes
On a midsummer night
Have driven us all to bed.
Swarming purposefully
Outside the mosquito netting
Next to your ear,
They hurtle in and zoom away.
The sound of their assembly
Is eerily resonant,
Like an air-raid siren.
Men live in fear,
And long for an unbroken sleep.

One mosquito, fainting from hunger,
At last finds a hole in the net
And sighs, "Heaven has come to my aid!"
Then leaps into the breach.
On such an evening
Some sleep peacefully
While others squirm.
The little fellows with a taste for blood
Choose their spot and make the most of it,
Or wage guerrilla war from all sides.
It's not unusual for people who go out at night
To sustain wounds over their entire body.

These nights everyone has a hard time,
Even the Great Jester above.
When daylight finally comes,
Multitudes rise from their beds and speak:
"Goddamned mosquitoes!"
Then resume three meals a day,
Until their turn to die and fall.

1988
Chengdu

December°

1.

"Hear ye!" The big lie shall blot the sky,
Two sparrows in the woods shall fall.
"Tibet," he says, "Tibet is fine and flourishing!"

The furious girl will not bite her tongue.°
Everywhere the monastic robe has lost its color.
They say, *It's to save our skin.*

But that one, oh,
The steaming blood poured out, the hot blood!
In the next life, who will grieve for him?

2.

Stormclouds! Doom!
In my mind's eye I see.

I know if I don't speak now
I'll be silent forever.

Sullen millions,
Lift up your hearts.

He was sacrificed once,
That man of deep red hue.

But as the tree of life is evergreen,
A soul is always a soul.°

3.

A worse defeat!
Thousands of trees, blighted as never before.
The little folk are quiet as a cricket in the cold.

The pair of praying hands
Was chopped off
To cram the bellies of kites and curs.

Oh, that rosary unseen,
Who is worthy with a firm hand
To pick it up from the slime of this world?

December 1995
Lhasa

14

The Panchen Lama

If time can cover up a lie,
Is ten years enough?
A child matures into a clever youth,
But like a parrot, mumbles by rote
The phrases that will please his masters.°

The other child, where is he?
The scar-like birthmark on his wrist recalls°
His previous life, before, when for ten years
He sat trussed with tight handcuffs
In some Beijing cell no ray of light could reach.
What bruises mar him now,
The child no one hears from?

If there are nine levels to the darkness,°
At which one are they trapped—he, and the other?
If there are nine levels to the light,
To which do they aspire—he, and the other?
Perhaps, in each phase of darkness and of light,
Where one is trapped, the other aspires.

Künchoksum! ° The world's turned upside down,
That the pain of impermanence,
Of samsara, has struck home to the Panchen Lama!

October 12, 2005
Beijing

Scream

A dream's about to end
But I'm still steeped in it.
I wish I could cling to that fading screenplay
(Like something whispered in one's sleep),
The air of unreality and detachment.
But the dream departs so fast!
Destiny, like a sword-point,
Pricked this fancy
Fate and time had knit.
In chill wind, whither page and pen?
It was a dream of moment.

I imagine I can scream
Such a scream, the heart will shatter in an instant
And in an instant heal.
Unbearable for all in earshot:
They will leave skid marks.
I would like that.

But how can I scream this scream?
I am no longer young
And am not without experience.
What's more, I look gentle and refined:
How can I scream uninhibited?
That's the sort of thing I used to do.
But the scream within the heart is terrifying
Because it never stops,
Each peal rings louder than the one before.

In this scream there is shattering but no healing:
No one can stand it.
To find relief I'll have to learn to let it go.

May 27, 2001
Lhasa

Witness to a Turn of Fate

Days and years, long time passing.
We seem to have reached the void. It is empty, hollow.

A turn of fate° rolls on, it seems,
But there is fear and sorrow
Like a bird startled, or a rat retreating. Black clouds swirl.

Much happened that year.° It's faded from memory,
Gone with the wind, gone with the wind.
Life must go on. How can your land of snow°
Survive a frigid winter?

February 19, 2006
Lhasa

Pallor of a Land of Snow

Among white pistils, she sees Dorje Phagmo dancing!°
No, not white pistils, but the peaks of high mountains.

Among pale flames, she sees Palden Lhamo racing!°
No, not pale flames, but the valleys between ranges.

Though the great hills ripple unbroken, and mandalas encircle
    the deities;°
Though blue lakes checker the land, and *trulkus* arise reincarnate;

Yet the white pistils wither abruptly, and the pale flames
    are as swiftly extinguished.
She swallows her grief: what news will she give Chenrezig
    so far from home?°

News, ah, news of the world, many a much-loved name
    to be tenderly mentioned. . .
But, Dakinis and Dharmapalas eclipsed, it crumbles
    to nothing.°

November 13, 2005
On a flight from Gyeltang° to Lhasa

I See a Fish Flying in the Sky

These days I always have to take this bus line,
So I know in my bones the sprawl of Beijing.
The bus I caught this morning was one of the midsize ones,
Crowded, but I couldn't wait for another.
Of course there were no seats, but I found a perch
    on the engine-box near the beefy bus driver°
And a panoramic view through the dirty windshield.
Only problem was a couple of air-fresheners there whose
    scent irritated my nose,
Triggered an allergy, had me coughing and gasping.
Behind me the other passengers were laughing hysterically
    at a skit on TV. °
I took out the book Tenzin had sent, *Lhasa Colloquial Reader*.
Ay! So many pages, when will I master it?
I read a few sections, imitating my mother's accent,
    and then something distracted me.
Looking up I glimpsed with a start, there in the gray drizzly sky,
A black fish in flight!
Of course I realized immediately it wasn't a fish flying up there
But a kite in the form of a fish.
Yet this kite had been made to resemble a fish so well
That it simply *was* a black fish, with many fins growing
    along the body
(The tail, in particular, was extraordinarily supple and lifelike):
I felt I had to consider it a fish.

I had to consider it a fish.
In that case, this was a fish that flies in the sky!
With a tremor I sensed a weird transformation in this moment
Which made this day unlike other days.

A fish swimming in water, a fish flying in heaven:
What exactly is the difference?
I recalled what they call Nonduality
In the Vajrayana of far-off Tibet.°
I remembered my dream of the previous night,
In which a Chinese Buddhist master, after ablutions,
    swung open the temple door . . .
Actually, what I mean to talk about (and have written
    along these lines before) is a serpent!
It's complicated. You can think of a serpent not only
    as a crawling animal
But also as a symbol. For example,
In a temple mural, monsters with blood-drenched jaws
    grip the many-splendored world:
One is a serpent representing hate and greed,
The vices which most easily infect mankind.
But there, painted above the head of a benign bodhisattva,
Behind the fairy maiden who looks like a mermaid with her legs
    tucked sinuously beneath her,
You see, like the blades of a gorgeous fan opened languorously,
Five tall snakes—soft, feminine, and tame,
As if they had honeydew in their little mouths.
A song comes back to me: *In your surroundings,*
Recognize Nirvana; amid the clamor, try to hear the truth;
For in the panoply of creatures, you shall see the Buddha.

April 12, 2005
Beijing

Dergé°

For my father

This scripture, also, vanished before sunrise on the Lesser Chill.°
I plunged my face in my hands and wept.
How could the horse I'd prayed for time and again, °
    which Fate made mine,
Advance into the hidden temple
As seven bones picked clean?°

Where shall a monk's robe floating in the air come down?°
Where shall my father live his life again?
Three sticks of incense,° a few burial-mounds . . .
O Dergé, my ancestral home, I wish it meant nothing!
Would that no road led there!
Aren't a myriad snowflakes another *khata*,°
An early welcome for this soul
Beyond the paths of men,
Among ghostly deer and white lotus
The perfect liberation?

My brothers and sisters, grieving, lose all care for life.
But O my soul, this side of the great bourn
You might as well wear one-and-twenty rings
When you fall prostrate: a glitter of silver
To light the nether world.

Auspicious streamers waft the hope of better fortune
    like a subtle fragrance.
In the next life, we shall know justice together.

The deep red village feels deserted.
A shattered echo brands a falling star
Upon my brow.

This woman whose once-tapering nails are broken,
—Eyes blur as phantoms crowd her mind—
Why is her grief so hard to tell?
Why should the cool tinkling of a bell stir up affections
    from the past?
Yet I, I will ride home on the horse of my destiny
Scattering *lungta* by the fistful toward the sky!°

December 25, 1992
Lhasa

A Mala that Was Meant to Be°

I.

Summer of ninety-four,
Leaving town at the turn of the darkest hour.
The field of stars lets fall
A hundred and eight beads of dew.
A woman whose hair is burnished at the temples,°
Clad in the garb of her race,
Will take the road to Amdo.°

(Easy to wear the local clothing:
It's part of a living tradition.
But how to inherit the grace of her ancestors?)

Omens are confused but suggestive.
At least three times
A young man from Dergé,°
Bearing an antique buddha in his hands,
Steps in front of you in the Barkor, asking:
Remember when you've seen this?

Moreover, when she and Venerable Nyima Tsering°
Stood beside the Jokhang's gilded dome, a palace in the
    background,
A gust of breeze made his dark red robe
Flap past her face.

It settled in her heart, an unexpected conversion
For this woman who had frittered away twenty-eight years.
O wind, in what part of Amdo
Will you gradually grow stronger?

II.

There's a place in Amdo with a tree
That has no equal anywhere.°

She lacks the root of wisdom.
She finds it hard to visualize
An image of the Buddha or
A letter of Tibetan
On a leaf.

Which monk was it, the placenta of whose birth
Was buried deep beneath the ground?
It caused a tree full of fragrance and symbolism
To grow there.
She imagines a lover destined for her.
In quest of this tree he will have come
From other provinces of mixed ethnicity
And found his way to her side.
He will think what makes the place unique
Is the green shade—an ordinary thing.
As he paces beneath the tree he'll wonder,
Will he bow down?
Will he gather the fruit that has fallen to the ground?
One hundred and eight seeds,
He puts them in her folded hands.

But "On his shoulders, which have endured life's hardships to the
    full,
Can he not stand the weight of a withered leaf
And know perfect emptiness for once?"°

III.

Damshung! ° It touches your face
Like a sudden, inescapable blow.
She bites her lip till it bleeds.
The pain of losing a father! The pain!
In the end, that sweeps away every blade of grass,
Every head of cattle.

A closet Buddhist, °
A fifty-four-year-old military man:
What were you thinking
In August of that year,
When you brought her and her littlest brother here?
Up yonder a place of pilgrimage,
Namtso.

"In 1991," she says,
Rolling a flower between finger and thumb,
"My life was ambushed
Among the bouquets and brocade that disappeared,
Before the gate of the house whose bustle faded day by day.
It had to start over, pathetically:
It really is impermanence." °

Actually, the flower in her fingers
Never bloomed;
Her poetry proved a curse. °

Uncanny . . .
At the peak of summer that year in Damshung, it snowed
    and rained together.
In an old tent
She huddled by the fire,
Couldn't stop sobbing.

Her father's face had turned ashen,°
Her father! Later, a lama divined °
That his soul had already been snatched by a demon in Damshung
But in the next life he'd be a *bhikkhu.* °

"Dergé, ancestral home!
Would that it meant nothing,
Would that no road led there!" °

IV.

One sees by moonlight here, a different moonlight.
The Tangla occupy the center of the leaf;°
In her thoughts they're dewdrops.
She can only look on,
No way to scoop them up in her hands.

The Tangla rise from the center of the leaf,
Soaring,
But they lack the brightness of home.
They go from sweltering to pleasantly cool.
As for her, this little brown bird flitting,
Her feathers are stuck together,
Her heart's racing,
She craves a few pieces of handwoven fabric.°

Tonight the dewdrops of the Tangla are transformed.
There are a hundred and eight of them.
A small figure with sunken eyes°
Suddenly grins, flashing white teeth,
Then hides among the silver ornaments.

Dressed in the garments of her people,
She senses something missing.

Among all these transitory relationships
He alone breathed the air of an earlier existence.
She yearns to find him beyond death and follow him;
Would that she had belonged to him in her youth.°

V.

In the dark night she is intent
On all her secret passions
That surge skyward from her fingertips;
Clouds whirl and shift kaleidoscopically.
Such is her life, unfathomable:
Is she sure she wants to call in
Those men with haloes?

How do they achieve tranquillity
Who seem to live in this world
But take a little house, filled with chanting,
As their only home?
Though her one kinsman
Is an invisible form,
She is completely ill-suited for that life,
Too often prey to all sorts of emotions
That wring her heart.

A man so rarely seen
Upon the dark red Way,
Gently ringing a cool bell.
Life hasn't scraped off his innocence.
Have you ever seen, hung in heaven,
The rainbow whose other end's in Paradise?
Shining jewel, lotus blooming,
Take pity on this woman
Huddled beneath a garish umbrella in the dust of this world,°

Always weeping for love
Like a jade bowl already full.
Fine wine is here!
But the bowl can't hold a drop.

Tibet's dark night
Conveys a promise, as a constellation
Might come into focus pointing at the heart.
But, beyond a great weariness,
What's left for her to say?
Though she embarks, once more, on a long journey;
Though she goes on living and aging.

VI.

In other provinces, mixed with people of another race,
Never long in one spot,
She tumbles into the clamorous dusk
And straightway the sprawling darkness
Is like a half-remembered face.
Love in the time of cholera
Is like hard liquor you can't hold
Or the heavy sound of tears suppressed:
They both fill your mind and are indistinguishable.
Nothing is left, nothing at all,
Except those hundred and eight beads
Of that particular oval shape and that particular dark hue,
Tied with that particular knot onto that particular yellow thread.
She cries out, almost in spite of herself,
"Oh, a mala!"
In her excitement she spills a glass of wine.

As long as it's Spring and the dewdrop
On a new leaf is pure,

And provided a woman is still growing up,
She can use that dewdrop to freshen her cheeks
And the neck that holds her head so high.
These days have brought a premature exhaustion
As she scrambles in a strange land,
Upon the paper of a strange land,
An anachronism.
Her haughtiness is suffused with melancholy.

"Here's a treasure that once was yours,
Before, when you walked a winding
Road, and the dust
Caked your deep red clothing,
Lonesome but untrammeled,
Tears sparkling clear,
The fingers of one hand working unceasingly . . .
Have you forgotten?
What is it you've grasped and won't let go?"

Outside the temple
Fluttering scraps of paper,° numerous as human wishes
—Such insolence!
They fly in her face as she looks up to Heaven with a sigh.

VII.

At the monasteries of Labrang and Ta'er°
She calls to mind a poet's words:°
"Eyes that last I saw in tears."
Her teary eyes have never crossed that line
To Death's dream kingdom; still,
She has glimpsed golden phantoms:
White Tara,° smiling at the corners of her mouth,

Golden Tsering Dorje, her father,
A monk's robe enfolding him!

(Using only her two thumbs,
The same that count the mala beads,
She lights a butter lamp
To celebrate good fortune.)

She makes obeisance as before,
But now more deeply moved.
Under the dazzling noonday sun,
The mala glistens white.
At Labrang, a fifteen-year-old *trulku* is no ordinary man.°
When he speaks a foreign tongue,
A kitten burrows in his arms,
A *vajra* knot to ward off evil tied around its neck.
But at Ta'er, she sees a breeze caress
A tree that has no equal.
Inside the gem-encrusted tower, a transformation: °
A hundred thousand Buddha-images,
Or one hundred thousand letters of Tibetan,
Morph into as many leaves upon a tree
As if settling on a pair of shoulders.
At these two temples (as at any other),
Her clothing blends unnoticed in the crowd of her own people;
But when will her long silence reach its end?
In this turn of the great wheel
She found herself encircled
By a mala foreordained:
Yet even though she pierced a veil of darkness,
A worldly rhythm almost steals her soul.

1994
Lhasa

Embodiments

At dusk en route to the Temple quarter°
A bent-kneed old woman shuffled along.
When I caught up with her I felt an inexplicable joy.
I turned and was astonished,
For on her face shone the beauty of mercy:
Who could be sure she was not some Shining One° incarnate?

But I remember, too, another evening.
For a better view of Mount Kailash°
I was hurrying toward the village at the mountain's foot
When a bent-kneed old woman gripped me by the arm.
Her hands were preternaturally strong
And she had the physiognomy of a vulture.
When I looked closely I felt a pang of fear:
Who could be sure she was not a Fiend incarnate?

May 27, 2006
Beijing

Way to Go

Your *Howl* of 1955 resounds off the walls of the Potala in this
  stubborn night with only half a moon.
Allen Ginsberg, the Yank! You smoke dope in a cramped room
  and contemplate the shadow of a rose in a place one foreign
  woman thinks ideal,
But it's an ideal this orphan, slashed and scarred and hands blood-
  soaked, might be willing to give up.
Were that full-bearded face a soft bed, that she could rest her eyes
  a quiet tearful moment,
Your golden body, bright and clear in an embrace, would prove
  of greater worth than gold.
In the power of your enthusiasm, tell her:
What lies ahead?

Scenes of dissipation have come to a bleak end.
Can I compare myself with Allen Ginsberg, reciting as he walks?
I'm like an angry evanescent rose—no, something smaller:
For sure he had fantastic imagery to draw on, a vast
  and potent store
He could unpack in radiance and say:
"I drink of myself, find words for what I feel;
Those words are wings on which I'll rise or fall.
But why don't I curse beneath this paltry half-moon,
Is it 'cause what lies ahead for me is . . . nothing? Nothing at all?"

Yet what lay ahead for Allen Ginsberg was a mother overwhelmed
   by illness,
Who scrawled her advice: *The key is on the windowsill,° under the
   sun in front of the window,
Son, don't smoke dope, live a good life...*

Be provocative. Goad them!

So must she mold her passions into art, and walk in a direction
   different from the crowd.

1994
Lhasa

A Vow

That night the moon was dim,
The moonlight streaming through his home.
He went far, wandering.
O god that dwells in moonlight be my witness:
I shall, in this life, meet him again.

Only because I keep in my heart
A rosary he left behind.
Oh, the hundred and eight beads
Are a hundred and eight longings.

That night the water of the stream was icy-cold,
The river flowing past his home.
He went far, wandering.
Spirit of the river be my witness:
I shall, in this life, meet him again.

Only because I keep in my heart
A rosary he left behind.
Oh, the hundred and eight beads
Are a hundred and eight longings.

March 10, 2000
Lhasa

Spinning Wheels

As the wheels spin round—whatever I'm driving—things far away
    come into view.
Those swiftly-turning wheels: Mitsubishi Tracker wheels, Beijing
    Jeep wheels,
Dongfang truck wheels, long-distance bus wheels,
Minivan wheels, red taxi wheels,
Walking-tractor wheels. And horses.
I count them too, because the sturdy hooves sport rounded
    horseshoes
So when they stamp the earth, ba-dum, the footprints
Do resemble wheel-tracks. And when people pass on foot,
—Especially when they go round a *kora°*—they trace one ring
    after another,
A track the soul's wheels score into the ground.
By help of wheels, I make my lonely way on earth.

All means of travel have a single name: stagecoach.
All places that we pass have also but one name: post-house.
Now, the imagery of stagecoaches and post-houses
    is classical. Still more so
The figure of the post-horse and the courier. Some say, to make
    a post-horse
Swift and tireless, give him sweet nectar
—The first fresh brew of highland barley liquor
Or holy water tinct with saffron crocus,
Made pure by a lama's word and glance.
This would transform my little mare
Into a racer good for a thousand leagues, a wingèd steed!
As for the courier, the messenger: in ancient times,
    on dusty roads,

He'd speed past, plying the whip, windblown and gritty.
Am I indeed a messenger?

Have I in my heart a letter still unfinished?
It's just begun; I don't know how to go on writing.
Does that make me a messenger bearing my own word to myself?
Or one who doesn't know to whom she ought to hand
    her message?
Or one in quest of a mysterious addressee?

> *Post road, smoking gallop*°

or

> *By crumbled bridge beyond the post-house,*
> *Lonely she blooms, and no man owns her . . .*°

Walking the roads alone, I'm a lot like a messenger.
But one who is a messenger in her inmost being does not generally
    require a partner.
For a letter to be treasured in the mind, you need a time of
    drifting solitude
To write, to add to it, to finish. Partners? One sole companion.
In all the letters to come, let there be only beauty!

With horses flying and the stagecoach racing, can the post-road
  · remember those who've passed by?
If the road were alive, its memories would be shrouded in
    billowing dust.
A messenger must travel light, and will have naught to show for
    his toil
But all the laughter and the tears.
Dust to the dust, sand to the yellow sand,
But what a heap of sand! So let the wheels roll on. The prayer-
    wheel in my hand,

Image of emptiness and illusion, spins ceaselessly from
    left to right,
And in its revolution makes me, too, into a *mani* wheel,
Engraved with countless runes to whirl forever in an
    unknown hand.
Therefore my name of former days has been retired: another name,
Fraught with exotic consonants,
Blazes up from an earlier existence.
I waver. I exult. I answer the call.

October 2002
Eastern Ü-Tsang and Kham

Lhasa Nights

O Lhasa, dreamlike nights!
A certain lotus may have never bloomed,
Sometimes a wineglass shatters at a tap,
Yet there are people, just a few—who blessed
Them with such spirit?—to whom this movable feast
Seems Paradise for banishment self-chosen.
If (imperceptibly) they weep, it's only
For a kinsman whom they couldn't keep.

O Lhasa, nights of woe!
A certain bluebird may have never chirped,
And sometimes garments are begrimed with dust,
Yet there are people, just a few—who spread
That plague?—who see bright fleeting Time as but
A pool wherein the posturing ego sinks.
Illusions countless, ever so seductive,
Can't lure a reincarnate kinsman back.

O Lhasa, nights like nowhere else!
A love there is that never came to pass,
And certain bloodlines gradually mixed,
Yet there's a man, perhaps just one—what kind
Of lightning bolt?—who makes a stifling fate
Serve as the hinge of reconciliation.
Upon the endless wheel of birth and death
I wish you would forever be my kin!

1996
Lhasa°

Serves You Right!

The blades, we know, surround us like a forest,
But see, there drips from each knife-edge the sweetest honey.°
Can't help sticking out our tongue to lick . . .
Mmm, such sweet honey!
Take another lick, and another lick, and another lick . . .
Oh, my tongue! What happened to our tongues?
How'd they get cut off?

October 3, 2007
Beijing

The Golden Season

It lasted days but only seemed like love. I see it ending now,
As sparkling dewdrops pass.
Peach-blossoms by the millions fall so soon, the tail of youth
  slips through my hands.
A man (in my imagination) has aristocratic airs,
But gradually he's going, gone. I wonder if his wife
  is gorgeous.
And that precocious daughter, would she be about my height?
Each day I inwardly exhort myself:
I'll know such love as others never knew;
I'll write such verse as no one else could write.
That's why the songstress clad in purple is not proud and
  does not sulk;
She's affable to every person of distinction—
Out of desire, or vanity, or fear of loneliness?
I long so much for you to embrace me as before
In Lhasa's deep night: dreamlike and woeful I have called it, a
  night like nowhere else.
The things that never found fruition have now all gone astray.
Yet I hear a stranger's voice behind you:
"Sunlight or love or wine, savor it while you may!"
So let us pass these fragrant days,
And saunter side by side through dreams of other lands,
Taking as real the opening of hearts, the touch of skin to skin,
Mourning together the deaths of those we love,
Seeking word from spotless temples of their blessed fate.

It lasted years but only seemed like love. I see it's over now.
Where long ago my wrists were cut, the scars have faded.
Peach-blossoms by the millions fall so soon, the tail of youth
  slips through my hands.

A man strives to paint what's in his mind,
Divorced from reality: will fame and fortune be his lot?
Will ruined buds know torment all their lives?
Each day I warn myself:
Don't live in a past that has just slipped away;
Don't live in a future not yet come.
How abstracted she seems, the songstress clad in purple!
Engrossed in her work, she yearns for drama:
Who could surmise this hidden tempestuous passion?
How I love these movable feasts!
I've said it as a toast: *May wingèd wine*
Soon change this woman's fortune!
Out on the prairie runs many a fine steed; the one she chose
    is not here!
If, wanton, I drink round the clock,
Will I know what hour life must end or start again?
Let all whom I have ever loved, or someday shall,
Convene beneath one roof in Lhasa's golden season.
As Indian music lingers in the air,
Light candles, pour the finest wine unstinting,
For then and only then shall we be perfect partners,
Surprised by joy. Outside
The rain falls, the wind blows, but we are young forever!

July 1996
Lhasa

Tsangyang Gyatso°

Lift up a wooden bowl in the night:
What hand poured this tea or mountain snow?°
When not yet sanctified,
Did that hand draw near these hands of mine?

The wind blows, the sacred streamers wave,
Whose voice is it that echoes in the hills?
When you join your hands or fill them,
When you put a hand by your ear as the other lifts high the cup,°
You yearn to speak but hold your peace.
Like a tree planted by chance:
Watered with tea (or snow from on high),
It won't grow up normal, it will be fragile.
I stand rapt and hold my breath.
From time to time a leaf drops down
And I lunge like a madwoman.
Clutched in my palm are broken pieces,
Tears on my cheek. It's enough.

What kind of hand holds fast a heart?
As some enchanted wren at night
Wheels overhead, it seems to trill its dying song;
The plumage scatters down to every land.

What is straightway reborn will not be you, the you of that flesh!

Yet I will lift in the night a wooden bowl,
For this tea or mountain snow still has not failed.
Lone genius, the canvas of the mind
Lacks but one brushstroke!

September 1997
Lhasa

Jotting Down Last Night's Dream

Coiling, tightly coiled beneath the water,
Tightly coiled among the huge stones beneath the water,
As a tortoise pulls its head into its shell
And the carapace, rock-hard, conceals the four limbs,
Like an embryo holding itself together,
(That's all it can do, hold itself together);
But the water rushing past is crystal clear.
Standing at the riverbank, the figure coiled beneath the water
    can see everything.°
This was my dream last night. I do not understand
    its deeper meaning.

May 25, 2006
Beijing

Tibet's Secret°

Dedicated to Tenzin Delek Rinpoche, Bangri Rinpoche, and
Lobsang Tenzin, who are in prison

1.

If you think about it carefully, what's the connection between
   them and me?
Palden Gyatso°, locked up for thirty-three whole years;
Ngawang Sangdrol°, imprisoned from the age of twelve;
Then there's Phuntsok Nyidron°, just released,
And, still captive in some prison, Lobsang Tenzin°.
In reality, I don't know them at all. I haven't even seen
   pictures of them.

It was only on the Web I saw, spread out before an old lama,
An array of handcuffs, leg-irons, daggers,
Electrified batons that can be put to various uses.
He had a hollow face, with wrinkles like ravines,
But you could still make out the splendor of his youth
And a beauty not of this world: for when he left home, still a boy,
He had to sublimate his outward charms to the energy of
   Lord Buddha.

October, outskirts of Beijing: winds of autumn sigh like
   a world renewed.°
I'm reading a biography I downloaded in Lhasa,
Watching the creatures of the Land of Snow trampled to dust by
   foreign jackboots.
Palden Gyatso says softly, "I have passed the greater part of my life
In prisons the Chinese built in my country." °
But there is still something in his voice "by which one can
   distinguish words of forgiveness." °

Every so often the masked demon shows its true face:
Not even ancient gods withstand it then,
But plain folk, born of flesh, can face it down,
Drawing on extra courage.
If any shout in broad day what they long for
    in the depth of night,
Or turn groans under high walls into a song and
    spread it everywhere,
They're rounded up. Extended sentences! Life terms!
Marked for death with two years' reprieve! Firing squads! °

I generally keep my mouth shut, since I know so little.
From birth I grew up to the bugle calls of the PLA,
A worthy heir of Communism.
But the egg laid under the red flag got crushed.
As one reaches middle age, a fury late in coming rises in the throat.
Tears, too, but only for compatriots who,
Though younger than I, have fallen into evil hands.°

2.

I do know two men charged with serious crimes and even now
    in jail,
Both living buddhas, both Khampas from the East:°
Jigme Tenzin and Angang Tashi, also known as Bangri and
    Tenzin Delek.°
(These are, respectively, their secular and religious names.)
Like some forgotten keycode, the memory of them
Makes a door swing open that stayed shut when I was in denial.

Right. It began in a post office in Lhasa when he asked me to
    write a telegram.
He said with a grin, "I don't know how to write the characters
    Chinese people use."
Bangri must have been the first living buddha I could count
    among my friends.

Once on Tibetan New Year's Day, we entered a photographer's
    in the Barkor
To strike a friendly pose in front of a gaudy backdrop.
I also had him brought in for Zhu Zheqin's music video, where he
    formed exquisite mudras with his hands.°

An Ü-Tsang woman who wore glasses became his partner.
The couple ran an orphanage: fifty kids, all little beggars who'd
    wandered homeless in the streets.
I sponsored one, but an unexpected event cut short my gesture
    of compassion.
I have no clue what they were arrested for.
There was talk it had to do with the raising of the Snow Lion flag
Early one morning in Potala Square.
But I have to admit, I didn't want to know too much, and I never
    thought to visit him in prison.

As for Tenzin Delek, on the banks of the Yarlung
    a few years before,
He watched an apple bobbing in the churning flood.
"See," he said, "A reckoning comes."
His fame had drawn me to him; his anguish left me at a loss.
He is of course well-known in this age of turncoats and silence.
This man, who made the rounds of the villages spreading
    the Dharma,
Who faced the government squarely and spoke out against the
    evils of the time;°
If he was "The Big Lama" to farmers and herdsmen, as well as the
    orphans he raised,
Still more was he a thorn in the officials' side, and they couldn't rest
    till they got rid of him.

They laid one cunning trap after another and finally ensnared him
    in the wake of 9/11.
Kill one, warn a hundred.

In the name of counterterrorism they charged him with possession
    of explosives and porn videos,
And with conspiracy to commit half a dozen bombings.
Yet I remember how sadly he had said, half a year before they
    threw him in jail,
"My mom has passed away, I will go on a year-long retreat for her."
Could a Buddhist who had made such a solemn promise
Have taken part in bombing, in mass murder?

3.

I also knew a lama who taught me passages of scripture
For my initiation as a Buddhist and for meditation.
But that day at Sera Monastery, his students were in tears when
    they told me
He'd been seized in the middle of a service
And police cars had hauled him off to the notorious Gutsa
    Detention Center
Because he had been implicated in some subversion-of-state-
    power case.
I drove out with a few monks to visit; the road, at that time
    unpaved, swirled with dust.
All we got to see, under the cruel sun, was the icy faces of the
    gun-toting guards.

He was released as abruptly as he had been nabbed: insufficient
    evidence.
Shaken by his ordeal, he presented me with a curious rosary
Made from prison buns and the bright yellow flowers blooming
    outside his window and sugar his family had brought.
Each bead was dense with fingerprints and seemed to retain the
    warmth of his hands
And the scriptures he'd recited through more than ninety days of
    humiliation.
One hundred and eight beads, tough as unyielding stones.

I've also met a nun just half my age.
That summer day when she marched round the Barkor, shouting
the slogan all Tibetans know,°
And the plainclothesmen rushed her and covered her mouth,
I was picking out pretty clothes for my twenty-eighth birthday.
At fourteen, I had had nothing on my mind except the
entrance exams
For high school in Chengdu the following year.
One of my compositions was devoted to the PLA who were then
fighting the Vietnamese.°

Seven years later, expelled from her convent, she works for a
sympathetic businessman.
She's petite but wears an unprepossessing wool hat, even in
the hot sun.
"Try a cloth cap instead," I suggested, intending a gift,
But she wouldn't agree. "I have headaches, the wool hat feels a lot
more comfortable."
"Why?" I'd never heard of such a thing.
"The way they beat me in prison, my head still doesn't feel right."

Then there's Lobten, a man I know slightly. He had an enviable
career, great prospects,
But once he stayed up all night and got crazy drunk, then took a
bus alone out to Ganden Monastery.°
The story is that when he flung *lungta* from the mountaintop,° he
screamed that fatal slogan several times
And the police stationed in the monastery promptly arrested him.
The Party Secretary's° comment: "*In vino veritas.*"
A year later, one more unemployed ex-con haunts the streetcorners
of Lhasa.

4.

I don't want to turn this poem into an accusation.
But of the people in prison, why are so many more wearing the red
    robe than not?
It goes against common sense: who doesn't know that between
    violence and non-violence there runs a great divide?
Just what you'd expect from descendants of an ogress:° we're glad
    to leave the suffering to our monks and nuns.
Let them take the beatings and wear a hole in jailhouse floors until
    they die.
You handle this, you monks and nuns, please handle this for us!

No way for us to know what racks the body and the soul
When each minute, each second is torment, each day and night is
    grim.
The body! I can't repress an inward shudder.
What I fear most is pain: one slap and I'd crumble.
With shame I count down their practically endless prison terms.
Tibet's true hearts beat steadfast in a Hell that's all too real.

Yet in the Old Town's sweet-tea shops,° pointless gossip fills the air,
And in its tea-gardens, retired cadres play mahjong gaily
    until dark;
In cosy bars, pot-bellied civil servants achieve a nightly stupor.
Let's hear it for jolly passivity! It beats being an *amchok*.
The so-called *amchoks*, 'ears,' are invisible informers.
A vivid epithet! Lhasa humor!

The selling-out proceeds quietly through watching and whispering.
The greater the betrayal, the richer the reward—enough to make
    you a bigshot.
An odd thing happened, once, when I was walking down
    the street:
I suddenly covered my ears tight, afraid that if I wasn't careful

Someone might wrest control of them
And they'd turn into *amchoks*, reaching out in all directions,
Ever more pointed, as in the child's tale where the little
    fellow's nose
Grew longer when he told a lie.

How many of the *amchoks* in our midst can be detected?
How many are unjustly shunned as *amchoks* who are not *amchoks*?
This twisted world is more devastating than 'sugar-coated bullets'
    ever were.°
These thoughts led me to a sad and reluctant discovery:
There's another Tibet concealed behind the Tibet in which we live.
This makes it hard to write any more lyric poems.

5.

Still, I keep my mouth shut, as I'm long accustomed to do.
There's only one reason: I'm afraid.
Why? Can anyone explain?
Actually, it's the same with everybody, I understand.
It's been said, "Tibetans' fear is palpable."°
But I'd say the air has long been charged with fear, real fear.°

It startled me when he began sobbing at the mere mention of the
    past and the present.
When the deep red robe covered his face, I couldn't help laughing
    out loud
To mask the pain that suddenly tugged at my heart.
Those around us rebuked me with a glance,
But when he lifted his head from his robe and our eyes met,
An imperceptible shudder let each sense the weight of the
    other's fear.

It was the night of the mid-Autumn festival when a reporter
    from Xinhua,°

Scion of herdsmen from north Tibet, his breath reeking
    with liquor,
Lit into me like the Party mouthpiece he was.
"Who do you think you are? You think your muckraking is going
    to change all this?
Don't you know we're the ones who make changes around here?
What are you trying to stir up?"
"Have I really broken the rules?" I wanted to retort, but in his face
    I could make out only the truculence of a lackey.
If more people make worse trouble than I did, will the answer be
    to jail or sack them all?

In my mind I hear those women gently chanting
"Sweet-scented lotus the sun's glare has withered,
Tibet's snow-clad mountains the sun's fire has burnt,
Yet may the rock of everlasting hope preserve us,
A band of youths who've pledged our lives for independence!" °
No, no, I don't want to darken this poem with political controversy,
I'm only wondering why the nuns in that prison, mere teenagers,
    are not afraid.

So one should write, if only that they be remembered;
And this shall be the author's pitiable claim to righteousness.
Of course I am not worthy. I'll be, at most, one who reveals at
    times her private thoughts.
Far from home, enmeshed in a race forever alien,
I whisper with some embarrassment from my place of safety:
Considering it carefully, how can there *not* be a connection
    between them and me?
Though I can only, through the meager tribute of this poem,
    show my concern from far away.

October - November, 2004
Beijing

Tears: A Final Song

for the person who walked with me in this winter's first snowfall

Snowflakes come down.
Snowflakes, dense and close, are coming down.
They shine like tears in someone's eyes.

Each one blooms warm,
Incredibly white.
Which one, I wonder, is mine?

From up above they pass before the sight
So quick, so light,
And vanish at a breath.

They come down, they come down.
Can see, can't count;
All seem the same.

Sworn friends all,
At last they rest,
Any- and everywhere their home.

They pile up slow.
A little pressure, and they turn to water . . .
That's what we're like, now.

Too many lives like that.
In time, the boughs will bend,
Some roofs collapse.

But it can't stand a spell of heat,
Much less the noonday sun,
Although it's coldest when the snow is melting.

The snow lands on our eyelashes
As if we'd wept heartfelt tears—
Who knows what for?

As fast as it came it will go,
Save on the highest mountaintops;
But that far up one can't aspire.

Now that the snow has ended,
It brings to mind last winter's snow,
That same continuous sound of silence.

March 1990
Kangding

When an Iron Bird Flew Past Shédrak Mountain

Exactly at noon, one day in September 2004,
I was descending with my Teacher° the steep, narrow path from
    Mount Shédrak. °
(This is a mountain four-thousand-odd meters high,
    in Tsethang, Tibet,
At whose cloud-wreathed peak there is a tiny cave
Which the sublime Guru Rinpoche° is said to have made
    his hermitage,
And the effulgence of his meditation lit up the mountain.°)
The joy of pilgrimage made me forget the toils of the previous
    day's climb.
I was proud of myself, for none of the monks with me could have
    believed
That I, of all people, would not only breeze through the hike with
    two full backpacks,
But pray aloud and be constantly snapping digital photos.
Journeys of a religious nature are usually cheerful, so it was with
    contentment that I turned my head
For one last glimpse of the cave festooned with five colors of
    prayer-flags.
Precisely then, a silver aircraft—no, an iron bird°—
Unattainably distant, flew over Mount Shédrak,
And with a flash it faded from the blue sky.

This was a startling sight. Had I not turned my head,
Then I would not have seen this iron bird fly over Shédrak,
For its flight was noiseless and swift.
It had happened in a split second and felt utterly unreal.
Had I seen anything? Yes. But what had I seen?
Mount Shédrak towered in silence as before, the prayer-flags
    were still fluttering,

You could still make out my countrymen robed in burgundy,
    striding with nimble grace;
But a moment earlier, there had been one
Of those shiny iron birds sailing past. It made me recall
The moonlight of the night before, outside a little temple
    with no name, where someone said:
A thousand years ago, Mount Shédrak had been the embodiment
    of a demon which kept growing till it almost pierced the sky.°
Then Guru Rinpoche, whose dharma power knew no bounds,
    revealed his wrath and
Vanquished it: nothing was left but the form of an enormous
    beast wholly tamed.
In our time, glittering iron birds fly past. What metaphor
    will they become?

September 2004
Lhasa

Strange Light

Can you ever go back to that place of shadow?
In this strange light° my long hair
Fades, strand by strand, as it slips to one side.

I'm not like the beasts that prowl everywhere;
Though their fur resembles my hair
They are sleek and glistening.
Round that palace (remind me: for whom was it built?)
A crowd has gathered once again,
Throngs of youths with great expectations.°
With bowed head I take my place among them,
Bearing in my hands a lyric
And twenty-something melancholy dreams.

Stream down, extraordinary light!
Ten thousand things depend on you for food
(A ploy of some Higher Power).
Whetted into unseen silver needles,
Your rays wreak invisible devastation.
When beauty fades and conversation falters,
It rises slow, the palace of the past,°
And I see him (or I think I do) who suffered in the flesh,
Dwelling in magnificence on high,
Defrocked, yet utterly perfect:
It's Tsangyang Gyatso°, perhaps twenty-five years old . . .
I wonder if he ever found the real shade.

Summer 1991
Lhasa

A Quick Note in the Small Hours

It's late, very late at night,
Soon it will be dawn.
No sign of the Sandman°, though.
It's not that I've insomnia,
I'm used to staying awake on purpose.
I'm thinking how to write my next piece,
The scintillating tale of a Khampa named Karma.
I've not only had a long talk with him,
I've promised to include him in the book, without fail.
But he is not the kind of man who's easy to write about:
There are too many stories about him,
He reinvents himself too dramatically.
A mere ten years can make him a different person,
Turning a *tsongpa* hustling nine-eyed beads°
Into a noted environmentalist and foe of globalization.
But I don't want to go on about Karma,
Though that would be even livelier than *One Hundred Years
    of Solitude.*°
Here's what I want to say:
I was writing the beginning of the story, leaning on a pillow,
When suddenly I heard outside a piercing cry of anguish
That should have jolted awake everyone sleeping in New
    Shöl Village.°
It trailed off into the sobbing of a young woman
Mingled with incoherent fragments of Sichuan dialect.
It seemed there was someone trying to comfort her.
This happened in the alley along the right side of my building.
I know many outsiders rent lodgings around here.
But so late at night,
On such a bitterly cold night,

This Sichuan woman, come so far from home to make a living,
What kind of calamity had broken her heart?
"May Heaven protect the well-fed masses";°
May the Blessed One protect, in this hour, that wailing
   human being.°
It was too late to stop my ears: I listened,
And Karma the Khampa had gone clean out of my head.

January 24, 2006
Lhasa

Dreamshadow

I.

In what hallucination
Did we meet, he and I?°
In that hour, evening flamed on the horizon
Like a red robe burning.
I saw his face, childlike
And stoical: he'd grown up
With stifled weeping.
Where do the teardrops fall?
On which faded page of scripture,
On what rusting vajra bell?°
Who could better understand
What's now a dream: the truth about our past?
But in the decade when the fiends rampaged
How he endured the utmost ignominy!

In this world of his that's wreathed in incense,
Deep wounds will still ache dully.
I'd like to see him smile,
A fleeting radiance,
A twinkle on that childlike face:
I couldn't keep from crying.

We must have some connection,
A vague one. No, why do I feel so sad for him?
The sunset gradually grows dim,
The mountains indistinct,
The world stands wordless and lonely.

How my prayers reverberate
Among these phantoms of the mind!
And at the core of every phantom form

There are more tears than prayers.
But I will still implore, under my breath:
O Lama, please tell if this affinity—
Predestined, though it came to light so late—
Is likewise of impermanence . . .

II.

For days, now, I am partnered with a fine steed°
And the wildflowers.
And there is you, my handsome young man, my clansman!
The mountains never end, yet there are echoes in the valleys.
The calm lake is crystal-clear, illusions flicker in the depths.
The pine and cypress, mushrooms, wild strawberries . . .
How could I forget that little golden fish,
The mystic rainbow,
The lightning that shimmered last night on the horizon!
Do you know?
I wish I could express myself in a language not of this world,
Like our mother tongue but purer, always fragrant:
Only then could I do justice to your generosity.
O my kinsman, many hills and streams away,
Why was it here, in this deep red land,
That we crossed paths unsuspecting? Tears stand
Hidden in my eyes. I bear without complaint the weight
Of an affinity predestined, which came to light so late:
We know it's there but don't know what it is.

III.

Gaze into a bronze mirror: the old days will come again.
That face, furtively restored at midnight,
On either side the sound of wordless sighing;
A strand of combed-out hair, as if this mortal world had
    somehow got detached:
I saw it in a dream.

Come spring, her little heart will bolt,
A skittish beast crisscrossing the wild,
Long-suffering, never crying out;
At last, in the season of swirling leaves
She'll let it slip away, the predestined friendship
That she longed for.

Close your eyes for an instant
And those lovely scenes flash into view.
No way to bring them back.
On the wheel of birth and death, in several lives already
We have missed each other.
I find the sadness hard to bear.

June 1999,
Kham and Lhasa

A Sheet of Paper Can Become a Knife

A sheet of paper can become a knife
—A rather sharp one, too.
I was only turning the page
When the ring finger of my right hand got sliced at the knuckle.
Though small, the sudden wound oozed blood,
A thread as fine as silk, and stung a little.
Startling transformation,
From paper into knife:
There must have been some mistake, or
Some kind of turning point.
This ordinary paper . . . a chill of awe.

October 16, 2007
Beijing

After a Few Years

After a few years
You're where we started
I'm at the other end.°
By plane
And car
I, too, arrive where we started.
After a few years
You've grown a bit
I've grown a bit
We look as though we'd grown up at the same time
Still youthful
Impulsive.

After a few years
I'm covered in dust
With a scarred face°
But everything's fine, just fine.
I wear a necklace of little skulls
To show my nonchalance.
After a few years
You look so neat
Scholarly
Could be seventeen
The tears inside
Glint like crystals
No hand could wipe them dry.

After a few years
Finally we sit down together
At first apart
Then edging closer
Surrounded by the clamor of the crowds
And jittering neon.
I want to speak but hold my peace.
You want to speak but hold your peace.°
What could we keep talking about?

October 1990
Chengdu

Return to Lhasa

It's been a year. I was somewhat excited about going home.
It takes only half as long now to reach Lhasa from the airport,
Thanks to two big bridges and a tunnel. The old Chushul bridge
Was guarded by soldiers armed to the teeth.
Traffic slowed, photography was forbidden, as if they were hiding
    military secrets.
But on the new bridges there are no soldiers ... don't they still
    need to be on the alert?
On both sides of the highway, identical new houses have appeared,
In Tibetan style (no glazed tiles!)°, and they're all flying the red flag
    with five stars.
I hear an inland tourist say, Tibetan citizens are so patriotic!
Yeah, right. If they're not patriotic they get fined.
    You unna-stand?°
Ha! The roadside shops are still selling fake palm trees,°
    fake cactuses,
Little fake zebras—it shows there's quite a market for these things
    in Lhasa. You doubt it? They've added
A new item: a pink fake lotus, look at that, blooming in the sun!
I saw the celebrated Qinghai-Tibet railway° on a concrete overpass,
And they say the Lhasa train station is not far to the right. In a
    few days I'll have to go see.
First I'll walk round the Potala. As I expected, the square has
    been enlarged
So that it looks even more like a copy of any public square
    from inland.
They've added a few more gates, brightly colored like wine-pots:
    Huge, imposing, incongruous.

In the afternoon, I strolled out for a glimpse of Lhasa's new look.°
At the corner of New Shöl Village° I suddenly felt something
    strange in the air.

It wasn't the dazzling sunlight, to which you might think I'd grown
    unaccustomed: it was *them*. They all had crewcuts,
Wore black suits or dark jackets and clustered in groups of three to
    five men. They were all wiry and young,
But with a tense expression, indeed a rather fierce look. They were
    muttering in the Sichuan dialect.
I counted roughly forty of them. A mafia turf battle brewing?
I had long since heard that Lhasa now has a Suining Gang and a
    Ganzi Gang, and so on,°
A cast of godfathers, bodyguards, flunkies, and molls—like a film
    from Hong Kong or Taiwan.
Ha! Lhasa had given me a revelation.
I was stunned. I wished I had a camera.
Suddenly a taxi collided with a three-wheeler.
That did it! A throng crowded round, and I jostled my way in too,
    and heard
The driver and the three-wheeler guy cursing each other out (in
    Sichuanese)
While someone tried to make peace (also in Sichuanese). But
    there was somebody else who chewed them all out
In Mandarin (quietly, but his face turned purple) and he seemed to
    have authority. He looked like a plainclothes cop
(Why else would the two parties have broken it up so quickly?)
    But in front of the Red Supermarket°
A police car braked to a stop, then a second one came, and . . .
Wow! Where did all the thugs go?

At 6 PM, riding my bike east, I feared for my life.
In the jammed avenues every kind of vehicle careened insanely,
Belching black exhaust, horns blaring.
I made it across Beijing East Road and reached the Jokhang
    Square. Was this the world of Tibetans?
Many were spinning prayer wheels of various sizes, unhurried,
Circumambulating the Barkor—turning to the right, as is normal
    for practicing Buddhists.

An old woman wheeled herself forward in a homemade
    wheelchair, reciting the scriptures;
A lovely young woman prostrated herself after every third step.
    I offered her a yuan° but she was very shy.
A young man with a black tassel on his head blocked the way,
    brandishing a strip of animal skin as he hawked his wares.
Oh, yes. That's become the vogue in Lhasa, to sew otter or leopard
    fur onto your winter coat.°
The crowded department stores offer a feast for the eyes, every
    kind of souvenir
Purporting to be distinctively Tibetan, but mostly from cottage
    industries in Linxia, Gansu.°
Pale-skinned tourists from inland are drawn to these goods; they
    believe cupronickel is "Tibetan silver,"
And take common stones for Dzi beads,° coral, and turquoise.
I know for a fact that two-thirds of the proprietors are Muslims
    with Northwestern accents:
If you don't believe me, go count them. A few Sichuanese are
    busy with bowed heads plaiting Good Luck Knots.
The craftsmanship is not bad, it's comparable to monks' work: they
    say even the monks come here to place orders.

But the sunset is beautiful, reflected in the deep-red Tsuklakhang.°
As if time turned back, Big Sister sits in the doorway still,
    her plump face creased in smiles.
She sells me a packet of butter from Nepal, the price unchanged.
As if time turned back, familiar lamas nod to me and smile:
You'd think I came every day at this hour to say my prayers.
As if time turned back, innumerable Tibetans form a line,
They come from Ü-Tsang, Kham, and Amdo,
They bear khatas and clutch paper money,
Holding aloft a lamp or a canteen filled with yak butter.
As if time turned back, I don't stand in line, but brazenly,
Like a tourist, walk right up to the Jokhang Hall.

Heads bob, figures sway, voices reverberate in the golden glow.
And I behold Jowo Rinpoche again,° and bending down in
    adoration I can't stop the tears.
As if time turned back, Tibetan countryfolk from all around, their
    hearts content,
Sidle past the hollow pillars closely spaced along the wall.
Tradition has it there's a lake beneath the temple° and the
    fortunate may faintly hear the lapping of the water.
So they exclaim: *Heard it with the left ear . . .*
    listen with the right . . .
It seems profound devotion, also, is transmitted from the left ear to
    the right.
When I try it, I hear only a wind in the abyss.

November 10, 2005
Lhasa

The Showers of 1990°

I wash my hands when it thunders.°
At the first raindrop, I mouth a silent prayer
And light the last brown stick of incense:
This overwhelming moment is my moment.

My moment is, amid the uproar, one of utter silence,
A fragile revelation only to be whispered:
The art of salvage,
Which some house of prayer may slowly teach.
I shake off the dust and listen hard.

How to escape this all-defiling rain?
At my back the seven passions and the six desires,
Rich, hollow, fleeting;
Before me, learned lamas
And renunciation.
Peculiar fantasy: on a single woman's lap
White feathers have fallen: so white, so many.

Composing on a rainy day, I wonder:
What paper should I use to catch the rains of Heaven?
See a world that money has remade
And all its lords and ladies: what shall be their fate?
They dance with demons, and they drink their fill,
And never guess the enormous secret.°

World-weary orphan, in literature you've found
A sweet dew that cannot be polluted.
It washes away all baseness,
Inclines the heart to that fond dream,
Escapist inconsistency:°
It makes you old before your time. Still, child,
However late, you will attain that dream.

How many showers does this body of Now°
Require to bear fruit quickly,° steadied on a single aim?
Perhaps in Tibet I'll be reborn,
Take my chance at union with the lotus.
I will press on and brave the rain,
Singing as best I can, or forgetting.°
I and some kindred spirits will care for each other,
And heed no more the call of family.

June 28, 1991
Lhasa

You Must Remember This °

"I can never forget Bajiao Street."
"Er, no," she says, "It's the Barkor."
"Barkor? OK, so it's the Barkor, then."
Circling the Barkor, you see the evening sky aglow;
Circling the Barkor, you hear low voices of entreaty.°
Keep them in mind, I beg you, along with all the rest.

"I can never forget you."
"Er, no," she says, "It is destiny brought us together."
"Destiny? OK, so it's destiny, then."
Recalling former lives, you hear choking sobs.
Imagining a world to come, you see the lotus blooming.
Keep them in mind, I beg you, along with all the rest.

February 14, 2006
Lhasa

Parents

Fateful mischance, that a girl (in the old order) to the manor born
Should meet, just when another flag unfurled,
A youth at ease with weapons.°
You two had three children.

All thanks to the State and to this ancient nation
Which can mix and match, like an artful tailor
Stitching a robe just right. The repercussions
Shaped your lives.

A monotonous marriage (neither was any good for the other),
A tiny home . . . Things got brittle.
Two rivers joined, the waters did not mix;
No war but many wounds.
A rickety building, doubtful from the start.
You tried so hard as it all went downhill:
Estrangement's daily grind, with no way back.
Your gift to each other was a life of regret.

I am your eldest daughter. I've a lazy streak.
You cling to me fiercely now as if to love long past.
Your illnesses distress me from afar.
I worry for my younger siblings, too.

1989
Kangding

Roaming the Infinite Night°

1. The People in a Deep Sleep

Invisible insects,
Flying here and there unseen
On black wings
With a dread virus
That makes eyelids heavy.
The whole land sinks into silent torpor.

What's gradually fading from our dreams and hearts
Is the prayer of old,
Or the blood-tie that bound us to You.
That thing that opens and shuts, that's called an eye . . .
Is it an eye?

These colors, shapes,
They're fake, of course:
We love such effects.
Even if abruptly disillusioned, we're still tickled,
Not like children who can't hold back their tears.

But where is it hidden, the eye of burning gold°
That shines when rubbed?
At dusk we want to go out,
But sleep slams down like a mountain.
Again we drowse and stagger.

2. The Hypnotist (*exempli gratia*)

There is another kind of sleep
For the nattily attired who can't stop yawning
As they turn us into marionettes.
A thrill a minute: schools of fish impaling themselves on the hook,
A dance in a straitjacket!

It's always the same gist,
But each one artfully reworks what others said,
Down to the tone and mien.
Placed by a different hand, the same stones
Will build a different house.
They think they're clever
To issue orders we obey
In lockstep, straining to model our sickness on theirs.
In truth, their kind of sleep
Is even harder to awake from.

As for a different kind of speech—we have long since handed that
        back to You,°
The path to Heaven, the babe abandoned here.
From time to time You call a name or two
—We freeze, struck dumb like mud.

3. To the Noble Blind

Let them stand and carry in their lyres,
With measured pace, in order,
Like grieving ambassadors.
They let fall a sweet-spoken dew,
But it comes to naught:
No lips are even moistened,
For what they have seen is not found here.

Blind itinerant minstrels, all of them,
Whose eyes ennoble this human world.
We, too, would fain enjoy Your love and favor,
And strive to draw close,
But we can't stop feeding vermin.°

Yet there is help. What they can see,
We too can see, and sing:
A phrase or two can stir the heart of a people.
Rivers divided would flow back together,
And reach by different paths a single goal.

To the end, we should pity one another.
We speak alike, we suffer the same wounds.
A cheer, then, for those who've been struck down
And sleep with Time, the Destroyer.
I yearn to go blind utterly.°

August 1988
Kangding

Nightfall on June 2nd

Twilight. Above that temple, how the sky gleams bright!

How long must a light shine before we notice?
Don't such buildings move us, religious or not, to a deep silence?

If it snows, the hills among this race of men will be transformed:
On what usually seems a mountain, objects grow by stealth
Until it looms as something altogether different.
We've never been able to call things by their right names.
A subtle change, a sudden ache in the chest:
Lucky for us it's far away.
The ache is like that temple: it rises gradually through years
    and days
Of prayer, until it changes unpredictably.
I see the silhouette whenever I pass by:
On top, the crouching deer are lifelike, with sad tales to tell. °

Should I keep this at arm's length?
I mean, after it snows, the mountains through the window look
    like another country.

As darkness falls, what's in the temple shakes me to the core.

1991
Lhasa

The Other Side

When you're near death
There's always an instant
When you poke through
That sheet of thin, thin paper
And your eyes (soon to close)
Peer beyond it,
Taking in the scenery
On the other side.
Then your gaze slowly comes back
In time for your last breath here.
The bystanders
Are all waiting calmly,
Willing to put up with a great deal,
Not like when I was fully alive and kicking
And they tried so hard to hold me back.
Maybe they'd still like to hold me back:
I don't know,
I don't want to know.
Basically, it's just one finger:
If a feeble effort
Can poke through that piece of paper
And find death,
The only thing I fear is that (surprise!) I might not manage to die.
I might leap from the bed
Screaming
Jabbing them with gusto . . .
Now *that* would be interesting.

March 1990
Kangding

The Illness of Tibet

The vegetation that I see on field and mountain
Is of three kinds, three kinds alone:
The thin and fragile plants are *grass*;
The brightly-colored ones are *flowers*;
The tall and straight are *trees*.
But to the lama's eye that takes in field and mountain,
Each blade of grass is only one
Of four-and-eighty thousand° kinds of grass;
Each flower, but one of four-and-eighty thousand different flowers;
Each tree, but one of four-and-eighty thousand kinds of tree—
Just like the Dharma. Of four-and-eighty thousand doors to truth,
Each way's the cure for one disease.
The illness of Tibet, when shall it be fully healed?

July 24, 2007
Kham

Come Home

In a frigid winter
A gale blew the prayer flags away.
The eagle of my spirit°
Was wounded by a demon,
Shocked into flight.
It makes me weep to think of it.

Many years gone by,
A great land thick with incense:
Where may the eagle of my spirit
Nurse its wounds?
That pained countenance,
It makes me weep to think of it.

Om mani peme hung,°
Om mani peme hung,
Come home.
Let the eagle of my spirit come back home.
Come home.
Let the eagle of our spirit come back home.

March 10,° *2000*
Lhasa

Positioning°

I'm not one to wander,
Don't venture out that much;
My rambling days are done.
Those far-off places
Teem with legend, but have nothing new.
Yet when sometimes a wing stirs in the mind
They vaguely feel familiar.
It's often better not to think too much.
You doodle on blank paper . . .
It's hard to forget home, and that's what'll get you in trouble.
Sending greetings is just a formality.
A few words prove what's possible;
What's habitual will pass for truth.
I'm not expecting much
And won't get out of line.
But what I feel, though hard to frame in speech,
Is eternal.

1988
Chengdu

Of Mixed Race

She's but the shadow of a dream whose tints have faded,°
The offspring of those poor and secret tribes.
In aching atmosphere among the peaks and swift waters,
She dips into her meager stock of adjectives
And lifts her voice, opens her lovely throat (much envied),
In songs that ring like gleaming golden coins.
Worth more than gold, her sacrifice;
But in return at least she wins a little joy.
Her brow is exalted with passion
Though her plumes are burnt by the setting sun
And one by one they fall away.
How gnarled her bones! Yet joy outweighs all.

Please grant a world of soil and stream
Where she may sing with pathos the anthem
She once improvised for no clear purpose,
That night of rebellion at the close of her youth:
Hot tears of despair made her lovely,
Annulled her earlier stance.
It shall be as a matchless crown,
Transcending all that might have made her fearful of this world
Because her calling is to be a shining priestess.
But over what rite of sacrifice must she preside alone
To ask, "Is it this?
Shall this one, too, be borne away?"

July 21, 1993
Lhasa

The Past

This snow-clad mountain, melting, is not my snow mountain.
My snow mountains are the mountains of the past,
Far at the sky's edge, holy and pure:
Many a lotus, eight petals opening,°
Oh, many a lotus, eight petals opening.

This lotus, withering, cannot be my lotus.
My lotus is the lotus of the past,
Enfolding the snow mountains, lovely,
Many a prayer flag, five colors fluttering,
Oh, many prayer flags, five colors fluttering.

The past, the past . . . such a past!
A host of divinities sheltered our homeland
As a lama keeps watch over souls,
As a mastiff stands guard by the tent.
But the host of divinities is long gone, now,
The host of divinities is long gone.

September 2002
Yunnan, in sight of Mt. Khawa Karpo°

Translator's Notes

Preface

some of the characters had too many strokes The official simplification of Chinese characters on the mainland began in the 1950s and had been codified by 1964, two years before Woeser was born.

Popular Cinema 大众电影 (*dazhong dianying*) had begun publication in 1950.

The girl who had been called Öser became Wei Se. The poet's Chinese name is Wei Se (唯色). Her Tibetan name can be transliterated in more than one way. She prefers to be known in the West as Woeser or Tsering Woeser.

minority nationalities. The Chinese term *minzu* 民族 was until the latter half of the 1990s translated "nationality" in official English documents of the PRC. Then the approved translation was changed to "ethnic group." A thorough discussion is beyond the scope of this book, but a few facts deserve mention. In both China and, earlier, the USSR, the Communist Party initially professed a high degree of respect for minority peoples such as the Ukrainians or the Mongolians. They were seen not as individuals composing a multiethnic society, but as peoples with their own social and political integrity. This was reflected in the policy of the PRC immediately after invading Tibet. In November 1950, Deng Xiaoping (then Political Commissar of the Southwest Military Region) issued a document stating:

> *The existing political system and military system in Tibet will not be changed. [...] All members of the religious bodies of all classes, government officials, and headmen will perform their duties as usual. All matters concerning reform of any kind will be settled completely in accordance with the wishes of the Tibetan people and through consultation between the Tibetan people and the leadership personnel in Tibet. Government officials [...] will remain at their posts . . .*
>
> (Shakya 46)

Before the Party gained nationwide power, its stated policy had been even more generous: the 1931 Jiangxi Constitution promised minority nationalities the right of self-determination and the option of secession. This promise was quietly withdrawn in 1938, and there is evidence that it may have been insincere (Moneyhon 129-131). But some Tibetans who joined the Communist Party early on believed that the Jiangxi nationalities policy, rooted in Soviet doctrine, would be honored in Tibet (Goldstein 30-32). The Chinese cadres who administered Tibet after the invasion had other ideas, however, and in 1955 Mao lurched toward extremism and centralization. It is striking that when the Tibetan Communist Phüntso Wangye was purged in 1958 (he would spend eighteen years in solitary confinement), a crucial piece of evidence against him was his possession of a copy of a book by Lenin, *The Right of Nations to Self-Determination* (Goldstein 227). My thanks to Robert Barnett for making me aware of this history.

her father was half ethnic Chinese Here, too, terminology presents difficulties. I will eschew the English term "Han Chinese" as either tautological or tendentious. A few scholars have argued that the concept of Han ethnicity itself is a late-nineteenth-century construct in reaction to the Manchu origins of the Qing Dynasty.

who had lived almost entirely in Chinese-speaking circles It may at first seem remarkable that a distinguished Tibetan voice raised on behalf of Tibetan culture today is not only speaking Mandarin, but by her own account has struggled as an adult, with only partial success, to learn the Tibetan language. Three points should be considered.

First, since the 1950s Chinese has been the language of administration in Tibet. Woeser's father belonged to the elite who governed the region for Beijing. That elite has always been Chinese-speaking, and indeed, until Chairman Hu Yaobang's reforms came into effect in the early 1980s, it consisted almost entirely of Chinese cadres.

Second, the education available to Tibetans since the invasion has been designed to facilitate integration into the PRC, *i.e.*, beyond the elementary level all instruction has been in Chinese.

Third, as early as the 1920s under the Republican government, the Chinese opened good schools in Amdo and Kham in a far-sighted effort to extend their influence in these border areas. Since education available under the old order was predominantly monastic, the only learning available to children growing up in the 1930s and 1940s who were not destined for the burgundy robe (and whose families could not afford a private tutor) was a Chinese-language education. Yidam Tsering, a prominent twentieth-century Tibetan poet, wrote only in Chinese. See Yangdon Dhondup (34–38).

She would later tell a reporter "Unfree thinker," By Paul Mooney, in the *South China Morning Post*, January 3, 2007.

the upheaval of March 2008 See Barnett ("Thunder").

Superscription

The verse from Milarepa, Tibet's hermit-poet born in the eleventh century C.E., is quoted from the translation by Garma Chang (40).

Remembering a Battered Buddha

Tromsikhang Market Barnett reports that "in 1993 an orange-colored concrete building had been constructed with 1,800 stalls, the largest purpose-built shopping center in Tibet" (72). At the outbreak of the unrest in March 2008, it was badly damaged by fire.

to buy droma The root of a fern plant, somewhat resembling the sweet potato and typically boiled for food.

a fragmentary chorten The Tibetan *chorten* is "a bell-shaped monument encasing relics and offerings, sometimes built for protection against harmful influences" (Alexander 319). What seems to be described here is a small-scale model suitable for indoor use. Woeser uses the Chinese word 佛塔 *fota.* In the photographs posted with this poem on her blog (http://woeser.middle-way.net/?action=show&id=117) it appears that the chorten was broken off at the base, and the beast and the Buddha are both resting on that base.

Had to be the Cultural Revolution   In 1966, the year of Woeser's birth, Mao Zedong appealed directly to the Chinese masses (and in particular to youth) to reignite the revolution. Initially, this seems to have been a maneuver against members of the Politburo who he feared might soon, in the aftermath of Mao's disastrous Great Leap Forward, follow the example of Khrushchev's colleagues and depose him. The movement thus unleashed soon spiraled out of control and led to hysterical cruelty and destruction on an epic scale. MacFarquhar and Schoenhals provide an excellent one-volume history of the political machinations. Chen Jo-Hsi recreated the epoch in unforgettable fiction. Jung Chang's popular memoir offers a vivid and personal insight into the era. Although exploration of this history is officially discouraged, some Chinese are trying to compile records while eyewitnesses are still alive; see for example the project of Wang Youqin at the University of Chicago (http://humanities.uchicago.edu/faculty/ywang/history/).

Although the Cultural Revolution proposed the annihilation of 'the four olds' (old ideas, customs, culture, and habits) throughout the PRC, the devastation proved especially far-reaching and systematic in Tibet, for reasons which Tsering Shakya analyzes (321-323). Tibetans' participation in the violence suggests to Wang Lixiong ("Reflections") that they were glad to exchange the gods of their religion for the new god named Mao; Wang has been sharply rebutted by Tsering Shakya ("Blood").

As a military officer in Lhasa, Woeser's father took many black-and-white photographs during the era. He was a good photographer and was of sufficiently high rank not to be challenged when he took pictures of mass rallies, struggle sessions, and truckloads of condemned prisoners. The negatives came into Woeser's possession after his death in 1991. Seven years later, after reading a book by Wang Lixiong, she offered him the photographs. He told her they were a unique and irreplaceable record of a history which some wanted very much to be forgotten. She then quietly identified some of the figures in the photographs and managed to interview many who were still alive. The resulting book, which combines Woeser's reporting with her father's photographs, is one of the best resources for understanding the Cultural Revolution's impact on Tibet. It was published in Taiwan as 杀劫 (*sha jie*, 'kill and loot'), with an English title "Forbidden Memory" for ease of reference. The Chinese title alludes to the fact that the term "cultural revolution", when translated into Tibetan (*rik né sar jé*), sounded like the Chinese words *renlei shajie*, "killing and plundering humanity."

Jiangxi A relatively poor province in southeastern China. The peddler was more than 1,300 miles from home.

wouldn't budge from three thousand Renminbi, that is. At contemporary exchange rates, this price was about four hundred (U.S.) dollars. On a purchasing-power-parity basis, it was about four times as much.

Let me Write a Poem

With a pen in my hand and your voice in my ears This poem may strike the Western reader as an invocation of the Muse, but there is no Muse in Chinese tradition. In response to an inquiry, Woeser said the figure being addressed could be considered one of the bodhisattvas of Mahayana Buddhism, or perhaps a Creator God, but in any case, it is exalted and omniscient.

like the herbs in a wine bottle Traditional Chinese medicine often packages herbs this way, steeping them in a bottle of rice or barley wine. One of the most sought-after is the *yartsa gunbu (Cordyceps sinensis)*, a caterpillar killed and transformed by a fungus. The harvesting of this herb has been a major source of income for Tibetan nomads.

On the Road

Woeser has reworked this poem a few times. The translation is based on the earliest and longest version.

A wish-fulfilling jewel This legendary object appears frequently in both Hindu and Buddhist folklore and iconography. The term is also an honorific title for the Dalai Lama.

December

This poem addresses the controversy surrounding the selection of a Panchen Lama in 1995. Tsering Shakya gives a careful account of events (440-47). Ten years later Woeser revisited the subject with "Panchen Lama" (p. 14).

Like the Dalai Lama (and in the Gelug sect second in rank only to him), the Panchen Lama is a *trulku*. That means successive holders of the office are acknowledged as successive reincarnations of the same mind-stream. Such a lama is identified in early childhood, within a few years of his predecessor's death. Often in the past the Panchen and Dalai Lamas have played a role in each other's identification and selection. The latter fact gave the Chinese government an interest in controlling the selection of the Panchen. They may have viewed it also as a test of the sovereignty they assert over all aspects of life in Tibet.

The previous Panchen Lama, who died suddenly in January 1989 shortly after giving a speech critical of the PRC's administration, had been revered for his efforts (while working with the Chinese) to champion his people, their language, and their rights. The "seventy-thousand character petition" which he addressed to the Beijing leadership in 1962, cataloguing the injustices visited upon Tibetans, remains a vital historical record (Barnett, *Poisoned Arrow*). His office, important in itself, gained authority from his personal charisma and the fortitude he showed both before and after fourteen years of persecution and imprisonment. The quest to identify a boy who would succeed him and be perceived as *being* him stirred deep emotions and became a major political issue.

In May 1995 the Dalai Lama announced his recognition of Gendun Choekyi Nyima as the new Panchen Lama. Within days the six-year-old boy and his parents disappeared from their home in Tibet. A year later, the Chinese government affirmed that the boy was in protective custody at an undisclosed location. Repeated requests by human rights groups and foreign ambassadors to interview the boy have been rebuffed. If alive, he is now more than eighteen years old.

In November 1995, a state-supervised selection process picked Gyaltsen Norbu, the six-year-old son of two Communist Party members. He was enthroned in Lhasa as the eleventh Panchen Lama in December, when this poem was written. Tibetans call him the Chinese Panchen or the Fake Panchen.

The abbot who had led the search committee, and who (with Beijing's permission) had contacted the Dalai Lama about the process, fell under suspicion of having communicated more to the Dalai Lama than he was supposed to. He, too, was arrested in May and stripped of his position in the monastery. His case was cloaked in secrecy, but he is known to have been sentenced to six years' imprisonment for "conspiring to split the country," "colluding with separatist forces abroad," "seriously jeopardizing the national unification and unity of ethnic groups," and "leaking state secrets." Rumors had him in solitary confinement at a secret compound inside a Sichuan prison. Around 2003 he was nominally released but kept in detention, and incommunicado, near a military base south of Lhasa. I have not been able to learn whether he is still alive. His religious name is, or was, Chadrel Rinpoche.

The political sensitivity of this topic compelled the poet to use veiled language. The translator suggests that the "two sparrows" who fall from their branches in the woods represent the two boys whose lives have been ruined in different ways; the "he" of the third line is the Chinese government; the "furious girl" is Woeser. "That one" whose steaming blood is poured out is "the man of deep red hue" later described as having been sacrificed: Chadrel Rinpoche. The pair of praying hands chopped off, which apparently dropped an intangible rosary, may also refer to the sufferings of Chadrel Rinpoche. Or it could refer to the interrupted lineage of the Panchen Lama and the challenge of maintaining the living traditions of Tibetan Buddhism when the leaders and institutions that sustain them are destroyed.

The furious girl will not bite her tongue In the original, "will not fast" or "will not go on a diet." In a personal communication, the poet explained that she meant by this a refusal to exercise "self-regulation." (自律, *zilü*)

A soul is always a soul (灵魂 , 就是灵魂)   Classically, Buddhism
denies the existence of the soul.   Consciousness is understood as
mind-stream, an energetic process both mutable and fluid: there is
no basis for the reality of the self as an entity.   On the other hand,
Tibetan popular culture recognizes the *bla*, the spirit that animates a
person (or even a place or a thing).   I cannot say whether Woeser is
revealing a certain eclecticism, or choosing to express Buddhist ideas
in non-Buddhist language, or relying on a Chinese word with a range
of meanings.   My thanks to Robert Barnett for flagging this line and
explaining the questions it raises.

Panchen Lama

For background, see notes to the previous poem.

The phrases that will please his masters. "The tall, thin teenager delivered a
10-minute speech in Tibetan that, according to an official translation,
dwelt on Buddhism's responsibility to foster patriotism and national
unity." ("Panchen Lama makes rare public appearance at Buddhist
conference," *International Herald Tribune*, April 13, 2006)

the birthmark on his wrist The tenth Panchen Lama, who died in 1989,
bore on his wrists the scars left by fetters with which he had been
shackled during a decade of imprisonment in Beijing.   It has been
reported that the presence of a birthmark on the wrists of Gendun
Choekyi Nyima was one factor leading the Dalai Lama to recognize
him as the eleventh incarnation of the Panchen Lama.

nine levels to the darkness Western readers will recall the circles of
Dante's Hell and Purgatory, but this is an old Chinese conception.
The Tibetan imagination similarly allots eighteen levels to Hell.   In
a personal communication, Woeser said that each of the eighteen
levels in her poem is a self-contained world containing both light
and darkness.   In this cosmology, the light comes to predominate as
one moves upward, but it was never wholly absent; and although the
darkness diminishes with the ascent, it, too, never wholly disappears.
Depending on how one understands the light and the darkness, each
of the contrasting descriptions of "being trapped" and "aspiring" is
applicable to either of the boys.

Künchoksum! As Woeser glosses in a footnote, this is Tibetan for the "Three Jewels" consisting of the Buddha, the Dharma (the teachings & practices of Buddhism), and the Sangha (the community of Buddhists). By a brief and solemn formula, believers "take refuge" in these three things. Here the word serves as an exclamation comparable to "O my God!" in English.

Witness to a Turn of Fate

Turn of Fate The word *lunhui* (轮回), literally 'wheel-turn,' can refer to reincarnation as the order of the universe (often in a negative sense, as a cycle that it would be a blessing to escape); or to one lifetime, or even a single moment if it is sufficiently significant. It is possible to interpret this poem as a reflection on the destiny of Tibet.

Much happened that year The choice of words (*duo shi,* 多事) implies that the things that happened were not good things. Possibly a reference to 1959, the year the Lhasa Uprising was crushed and the Dalai Lama fled to India.

How can your land of snow / Survive a frigid winter? The "you" may be the Dalai Lama.

Pallor of a Land of Snow

Dorje Phagmo: also Vajrayogini, a female tutelary goddess who assumes several forms in Indian and Tibetan tantric Buddhism. In sacred art she is always painted a bright red color, and often appears as the consort of Chakrasamvara. See Simmer-Brown 141-144. There is also a line of female *trulkus* enduring from the fifteenth century to the present day, the abbesses of Samding Monastery near Yamdrok Lake, about 60 miles southwest of Lhasa. These *trulkus* are honored as emanations of Dorje Phagmo.

Palden Lhamo, the only female among the Dharmapalas, is considered the protectress of Tibet and the Dalai Lamas.

mandalas For an explanation of the role of mandalas in tantric Buddhism, see Powers 227-229. A practice that has become widely known is "sand-painting," in which a mandala is painstakingly created from colored sands, briefly contemplated, then peacefully destroyed.

Chenrezig: the Tibetan name for the Buddha of Compassion whose Sanskrit name is Avalokiteshvara. Tibetans believe that the Dalai Lama makes Chenrezig manifest, and their exiled leader is sometimes referred to under that name.

Dakinis: energetic goddesses, often wrathful, usually depicted garlanded in skulls. The Tibetan word is *Khandroma*, meaning 'sky-dancer' or 'one who traverses the void.' An elaborate mysticism has developed around the figure of the Dakini. For a detailed and sympathetic analysis, see Simmer-Brown.

Dharmapalas: eight wrathful divinities, all but one of them male. The name means Protectors of the Law. In Tibetan, *drak shé.*

A flight from Gyeltang Woeser uses the old Tibetan name for the city in Yunnan known to most Chinese as Zhongdian. In 2001, the city was officially renamed Shangri-la (*Xiang ge ri la*) in a bid for tourism.

I See a Fish Flying in the Sky

I found a perch on the engine-box This bus design, in which the engine is housed in a box that takes up space inside the passenger compartment (usually next to the driver) is more common in Asia than in North America.

laughing hysterically at a skit on TV Most Beijing buses have been outfitted with video screens.

what they call Nonduality / In the Vajrayana of far-off Tibet. Nonduality is a doctrine rooted in the Hindu scriptures and shared by all schools of Buddhism. Put simply, it holds that the distinction between subject and object is illusory and many other distinctions are illusory as well.   In American literature it was pithily set forth by Ralph Waldo Emerson in his poem of 1857, "Brahma," which begins:

If the red slayer think he slays,
Or if the slain think he is slain,
They know not well the subtle ways
I keep, and pass, and turn again.

Far or forgot to me is near,
Shadow and sunlight are the same,
The vanished gods to me appear,
And one to me are shame and fame.

Vajrayana, the "diamond vehicle," denotes the religion which came to dominate Tibetan culture from the seventh century C.E.: Mahayana Buddhism with an infusion of Indian tantra. The tantra is a system of yogic meditation and ritual (largely esoteric) embraced in the belief that it accelerates spiritual transformation. By urging engagement on behalf of suffering beings (the bodhisattva ideal) and commending pleasure as a means to enlightenment (an easily-misunderstood aspect of the tantra), Vajrayana could be taken to qualify the principle of nonduality.

Dergé

Dergé is a remote Khampa town (in 1992, it was still accessible only by a dirt road) close to the border between the Tibet Autonomous Region and the Tibetan areas of Sichuan. It was the birthplace of Woeser's father, Tsering Dorje.

This scripture, also, vanished Since early in the eighteenth century, Dergé has had a printing house and a library which made it a center of monastic learning. These institutions were slated for destruction during the Cultural Revolution. The dramatic tale of how they survived largely unscathed is recounted by Ricard in a chapter that includes fine photographs of a uniquely Tibetan technology of book-making (142-143). A somewhat different account by Tenzin Choephel ("The Survival of Dérgé Parkhang Chenmo") is posted at http://www.tibetwrites.org.

The Lesser Chill The penultimate of 24 seasonal division points in the Chinese year. The Lesser Chill occurs in early January, and the term is here used approximately. Woeser's father died on December 25, 1991.

How could the horse I'd prayed for Woeser was born in the Year of the Horse and often uses that animal to represent herself or her personal destiny. That the horse was the object of repeated prayer is meant to suggest her innermost self.

As seven bones picked clean In a personal communication, Woeser explained that she is suggesting purification, the process of becoming more spiritual.

Where shall a monk's robe floating in the air come down? As she mentions in "A Mala that Was Meant to Be," Woeser consulted a medicine lama soon after the death of her father, who had been an officer in the PLA. The lama performed a divination and said that her father would be reincarnated as a monk. The robe referred to (袈裟, *jiasha*, from the Sanskrit *kasaya*) is the simple outer garment of a Buddhist monk, traditionally made of patchwork as a sign of detachment and poverty.

Three sticks of incense The traditional Chinese practice of bowing (拜拜, *baibai*) in ancestor-worship prescribes that the worshipper should hold either one or three sticks of incense in one hand.

Aren't a myriad snowflakes another khata The khata is a white silk scarf used as a ceremonial gift not only at arrivals and departures, but also at weddings and funerals and other occasions calling for expressions of goodwill.

Scattering lungta by the fistful toward the sky The Tibetan word *lungta* means literally "wind horse," a motif in folklore that took several forms. Here and in "Tibet's Secret" (p. 47) it denotes a stack of square pieces of paper, often of different colors, on each of which a prayer has been written. Tibetans will cast these like confetti from high places such as mountain passes—often with the cry *Lha gyal lo*,

'Victory to the gods.' The mood can be one of celebration, prayer, or hope for the future.

A Mala that Was Meant to Be

Or "Predestined Rosary." The poem recounts a journey Woeser made when, haunted by thoughts of her father (who had died almost three years before), she felt increasingly drawn toward the Buddhist religion. She recalls leaving Lhasa in the predawn darkness and driving through the Tangla mountain range to visit two famous monasteries. In a personal communication in the autumn of 2007, she elaborated on the experiences which the poem treats in an occasionally cryptic and allusive fashion. Those explanations are included in the following notes.

Mala Strings of beads facilitate the counting of prayers and chants in several religions; as so often, the roots lie in Hinduism. Woeser uses the Chinese word for Buddhist prayer beads, 念珠 *nianzhu*, but in this poem the object epitomizes Tibetan religious culture. The Tibetan word is *drengwa*; for this poem I have used the Sanskrit word *mala* because it is more familiar in English. In Tibetan Buddhism, the mala is used to count short *mantras* without distraction; its use is somewhat different from that of the Roman Catholic rosary, in which sets of prayers are repeated by one who contemplates a series of themes. A variety of mathematical, scriptural, and astronomical explanations have been suggested for the mala's number of beads, which (as the poem mentions repeatedly) is 108.

A woman whose hair is burnished at the temples She had dyed a couple of golden highlights into her black hair.

the road to Amdo See Geographical Note.

Dergé was the birthplace of her father and was associated, in her mind, with his death.

Venerable Nyima Tsering In a chapter of *Notes on Tibet*, Woeser wrote sympathetically about a stressful trip this cleric made to Norway, where he found himself caught between the expectations of Tibetan exiles and his minders from the PRC. As "Nyima Tsering's Tears," this chapter has been translated into English by Tenzin Losel, Bhuchung D. Sonam, Tenzin Tsundue, and Jane Perkins and is available at http://www.tibetwrites.org. Nyima Tsering figures in this poem because he blessed a *mala* for Woeser.

a tree / That has no equal anywhere. At the monastery of Kumbum, known in Chinese as Ta'er Si, there is a sandalwood tree which is believed to have sprung (or to be descended from a tree that sprang) from the spot where the placenta of Tsongkhapa fell to earth when he was born. Tsongkhapa founded the Gelug sect early in the fifteenth century C.E. The tradition to which Woeser alludes holds that on each leaf of this tree, the faithful can discern either a letter of the Tibetan alphabet or an image of the Buddha. The name 'Kumbum' signifies 'one hundred thousand' in Tibetan and refers to the number of leaves on the tree.

But "On his shoulders . . ." The quotation is taken from a short story Woeser published in 1992, 幻影幢幢 (*Flickering Shadows of Illusion*, in *Xizang Wenxue* Vol. 122, No. 5, pp. 4 - 11) There the reference is to a lover who disappoints. For the poem, she made the excerpt from the story slightly more concise.

Damshung A county north of Lhasa and south of the holy lake Namtso, populated largely by nomads. Tsering Dorje fell ill before he could visit the lake.

A closet Buddhist Woeser's first inkling that her father, a deputy commander (副司令员 *fu silingyuan*, roughly equivalent to a lieutenant general; see Mulvenon and Yang 32) in the PLA, might harbor Buddhist faith came when she was home during a break from college in the 1980s. The Panchen Lama visited the house as part of his effort to meet local Tibetans in positions of authority. She remembers her astonishment when her father (who was wearing his dress uniform) went down on one knee before the Panchen Lama. Later, she realized that trips on which he had taken her mother, ostensibly for her health, had all been pilgrimages.

It really is impermanence. Chinese 无常 *wu chang,* Tibetan *mi takpa,* Sanskrit *anitya.* A key concept of Buddhism, implying not merely temporal limitation but the idea that things do not exist "from their own side," of themselves.

Her poetry proved a curse. That year Woeser had written a number of stories and poems with tragic endings and doomed protagonists. When her father was stricken (he died in December of that year), she wondered if her recent writings had brought this misfortune about.

Her father's face had turned ashen His illness, which proved fatal, was brought on by altitude sickness.

a lama divined Woeser consulted a medicine lama, who performed a divination by pouring sand on the ground.

in the next life he'd be a bhikkhu. Woeser uses the Tibetan word *gelung,* which translates the Sanskrit *bhikshu,* denoting a fully ordained Buddhist monk. English-speaking readers are likely to be familiar with the Pali form, *bhikkhu.*

"Dergé, ancestral home!" These lines come from "Dergé" (p. 20).

The Tangla occupy the center of the leaf Comparing the Tangla Mountains to "beads" of dew continues the *mala* imagery. That these dewdrops are imagined on a "leaf" may have a similar motivation: the leaves of the sandalwood tree at Ta'er Si are invoked at the close as a touchstone of faith.

She craves a few pieces of handwoven fabric In a personal communication, Woeser explained that she finds comfort in collecting Tibetan handicrafts.

A small figure with sunken eyes Here and a few lines later (*He alone breathed the air of an earlier existence*) she is thinking of the Venerable Nyima Tsering. But—not entirely consciously—her father may also be included in these references.

Would that she had belonged to him in her youth i.e., had been devout from her childhood.

Huddled beneath a garish umbrella A self-deprecating description which may hint at spiritual potential: the *parasol* is one of the Eight Auspicious Symbols of Buddhism.

fluttering scraps of paper Her own poems and the literary ambition that propels them.

Labrang and Ta'er Labrang Tashikyil Monastery is a large monastic center of learning founded early in the 18th century in a valley about 100 miles southwest of Lanzhou in Gansu Province. Gyurme Dorje reports "it is among the handful anywhere in Tibet that survived the Cultural Revolution relatively intact" (627). Ta'er Monastery, known to Tibetans as Kumbum Jampaling, stands less than twenty miles southwest of Ziling (Chinese: Xining), the capital of Qinghai. It dates from the sixteenth century and has suffered a more difficult history in recent times. Since 1998 the abbot, Arjia Rinpoche, has been living and teaching in the United States.

she calls to mind a poet's words Alluding to the beginning of T. S. Eliot's poem "Eyes that last I saw in tears":

> Eyes that last I saw in tears
> Through division
> Here in death's dream kingdom
> The golden vision reappears
> I see the eyes but not the tears
> This is my affliction
>
> (Eliot 133)

White Tara Together with Green Tara (who is visualized as younger and more active), White Tara is a central figure in the devotions of Vajrayana Buddhism. In some contexts, she is honored as a goddess; in others, she is contemplated as a feminine archetype leading the practitioner to develop his or her full potential. The medicine lama whom Woeser consulted after her father's death said that White Tara was Tsering Dorje's tutelary deity.

a fifteen-year-old trulku is no ordinary man Perhaps written with tongue in cheek. Woeser recalls that when the young man tried to say something in English, the cat in his arms became agitated and they joked that his cat must understand English.

Inside the gem-encrusted tower At Kumbum a four-story temple was built around the famous tree, some of whose dead branches are still on display there. One might contrast the inspiration Woeser felt with the reaction of Patrick French, who found Kumbum "a warped and petrified theme-park" (81-83). Perhaps what moved Woeser was something that was no longer there. Compare the line in "Strange Light" (p. 55), "It rises slow, the palace of the past," which she explains as a reference to the Potala, "but not as it exists today."

Embodiments

the Temple quarter Woeser uses the Tibetan word *Kora*, "circular road," which appears in the names of both the Barkor (which surrounds the Jokhang Temple) and the Lingkor (which encompasses a larger area including the Potala). Synecdoche for the old center of Lhasa.

some Shining One One of the bodhisattvas venerated in Mahayana Buddhism for their power as well as their example of compassion.

Mount Kailash A Himalayan mountain at the western edge of Tibet, close to the Indian border. It is the destination of many pilgrims because it is sacred to several religions. It has never been climbed.

Way to Go

The key is on the windowsill In the Chinese translation on which Woeser relied (here rendered literally into English), the key which Ginsberg's mother beheld in her last vision seems to have undergone a sea change into something tangible and practical. The reference is to "Kaddish," where Ginsberg quotes a letter from his schizophrenic mother Naomi (at that time confined in a psychiatric facility) which he received after her death:

Strange prophecies anew! She wrote—'The key is in the
window, the key is in the sunlight at the window—
I have the key—Get married Allen don't take drugs—
the key is in the bars, in the sunlight in the window.
Love,
                                                    your mother'
which is Naomi—
                                            (Ginsberg 108)

Ginsberg mentions this key three other times in "Kaddish." It can be
understood as a spiritual insight that had long eluded his tormented
mother but that came to her, at the end, with a promise of freedom
and peace.

Spinning Wheels

walking-tractor wheels The walking tractor or walk-behind tractor is
perhaps more familiar in Europe and Asia than in North America. It
resembles a powerful push lawnmower.

especially when they go round a Kora. The Tibetan word denotes a
circumambulation path. The practice of walking round a sacred
place (perhaps a prescribed number of times) is observed in many
religions. It is is prominent in both Tibetan Buddhism and Bön,
the indigenous religious tradition of Tibet, though the two religions
prescribe opposite directions for circling their shrines.

Post road, smoking gallop A now-common phrase traceable to a poem
by Kong Zhigui, "Proclamation on North Mountain." (5th century
C.E.)

By crumbled bridge beyond the post-house . . . A quotation from "Ode to
the Plum Blossom," a work by Lu You (12th-13th century C.E.)

Lhasa Nights

Six years after moving back to the city of her birth, the poet
interweaves images of personal incompletion with a veiled tribute to
a distinguished former resident of the Potala.

Serves You Right!

The image of "honey on a razor's edge" comes from Chapter 7 of the eighth-century *Bodhisattvacharyavatara*, by Shantideva, where it represents sensual pleasures whose pursuit brings pain. Woeser's emphasis on the loss of the tongue suggests a sociopolitical application in which the enjoyment of material or pecuniary rewards must be weighed against the loss of freedom of expression.

Tsangyang Gyatso

Tsangyang Gyatso Born 1683 in the southern forests of the Monpa region on the outskirts of Tibet (today, the disputed territory of Arunachal Pradesh, claimed by both China and India but controlled by India), this sensitive boy was identified as the sixth incarnation of the Dalai Lama and trained in secrecy and seclusion while his predecessor's death was concealed for fifteen years. When he was finally brought to Lhasa to assume his office, he refused to live as a monk. His inclinations were to beer, women, and song, about which he wrote between sixty and seventy poems in vernacular Tibetan. These verses achieved the status of classics in a culture whose literature was otherwise predominantly religious, and they have been set to music many times. The young man assumed his responsibilities in an era of acute political stress. He was kidnapped by a Mongol warlord who intended to take him as a captive to China. He died en route, south of Lake Kokonor, in his twenty-sixth year. The inner conflicts he candidly recorded have done nothing to diminish the reverence with which Tibetans honor his memory. That is partly because it is possible to interpret the love-poems allegorically and discern a political satire targeting the Regent (Sørensen 25, with examples *passim*); they also contain suggestions that the Dalai Lama's liaisons, far from being a weakness of the flesh, were exercises in karmamudrā sexual yoga (Simmer-Brown 222), though Aris dismisses the latter hypothesis as a "pious justification" (160).

As for this poem, in a personal communication the author mentioned that the tea and the snow from the mountaintop symbolize Tibetan culture, and make one who is nourished by them both beautiful and vulnerable. The delicate hands of Tsangyang Gyatso are compared to the branches of a fragile tree. He is imagined making the gesture of a bard about to sing because he was a poet. She also said that when a lama bestows the water poured for tea, or blesses it, the tea is believed to impart strength.

this tea Tibetans consider tea (even when made without butter) a characteristically Tibetan drink, although it is at least equally a characteristically Chinese drink. In Tibet it is usually made from a tea brick, as was the style in China before the Ming dynasty.

When you put a hand by your ear In Tibet, a singer thus signals the start of a performance.

Jotting Down Last Night's Dream

Standing at the riverbank, the figure coiled beneath the water The dreamer experienced the scene from the point of view both of the creature under the water and of a person standing at the water's edge. In a personal communication, the poet explained that such dual standpoints are common in her imagination.

Tibet's Secret

This poem (西藏的秘密, *xizangde mimi*) has also been translated by a team consisting of Susan Chen, Jane Perkins, Buchung D. Sonam, Tseten Gya, Phuntsok Wangchuk, Sangjey Kyap, and Tenzin Tsundue. I have relied on their work for the rendering of Tibetan proper names. Under the title "Secret Tibet," their version is available at http://www.tibetwrites.org.

Woeser wrote footnotes explaining a few details for Chinese readers. I have incorporated some of that material into the notes below while indicating its source.

Palden Gyatso [Woeser's footnote:] "An ordinary Tibetan monk. After the Lhasa Uprising in March 1959 (when he was 28 years old), he was imprisoned because he refused to betray his teacher. Later, the sentence was extended without a break and he was subjected to extreme forms of torture. Only in 1992, at the age of 60, was he released. After that, he fled to India, to the Dalai Lama's seat at Dharamsala. There he wrote for the world a memoir of his ordeal, *Fire Under the Snow.*"

Ngawang Sangdrol [Woeser's footnote, with date of release corrected:] "An ordinary Tibetan nun. In 1990, when only 12 years old, she was arrested and jailed for taking part in a protest march in Lhasa. She thus became the youngest political prisoner in Tibet. Nine months later she was released. But she was arrested again for taking part in a demonstration in 1992, and she spent 11 years behind bars. While in prison, she and 13 other nuns composed songs about prison life and recorded them with a smuggled tape-recorder which they later managed to get to the outside world, causing a tremendous stir. They were called "the singing nuns." As a result of intense protest from the international community, in October 2002 she was released ten years early, her health much impaired."

Phuntsok Nyidron: Another of the Drapchi nuns, sentenced in 1989 to nine years' imprisonment for "counter-revolutionary propaganda inciting to crime." Woeser notes that she was the last of the nuns to be set free, in February 2004.

Lobsang Tenzin [Woeser's footnote, date of riot corrected:] "A man of Lhasa, born in 1966. Before his arrest he was a sophomore in the Tibetan Literature Department at Tibet University. He was accused of murdering a member of China's Armed Police on March 5, 1988, in the so-called Lhasa Riots. Although there was no evidence connecting him with this case, he was sentenced to death with a two-year suspension. As a result of international pressure, this was commuted to life imprisonment and later reduced to 18 years. As of 2004, he still has to serve 10 years, and is at present locked up in Pomé County Prison in Nyingtri Prefecture. This is a prison that specializes in the incarceration of major political prisoners; of twenty-five inmates, one has gone insane. On account of the vicious beatings he has received, Lobsang Tenzin has suffered damage to his heart and kidneys and cannot stand upright. He experiences spells of blindness and frequent violent headaches. Many are concerned, in view of his physical condition, that he won't make it to 2014."

In the spring of 1991, Lobsang Tenzin was still in Drapchi Prison when U.S. Ambassador James Lilley was allowed to visit there and meet with individuals whom the State Department classified as political prisoners. Two of them wrote a letter describing abuse and torture inside the prison and gave it to the ambassador. A few seconds later, a guard snatched it from his hand and prison officials refused to give it back. Lobsang Tenzin was one of the authors of the letter. He was immediately put in solitary confinement and soon was transferred to Pomé County Prison, which stands about 200 miles east of Lhasa and supplies forced labor to the logging industry. He has more recently been transferred to Quxu (Chushul) Prison, south of Lhasa.

The People's Armed Police, also called "China's Armed Police," is a paramilitary organization tasked with internal security, reporting both to the Ministry of Public Security and to the Central Military Commission. Estimates of the size of its staff range from 660,000 to 1.5 million. The *wujing*, as they are known by abbreviation, are typically deployed instead of ordinary police to suppress demonstrations in Tibet.

like a world renewed The phrase occurs in poetry ranging from Cao Cao to Mao Zedong. Woeser had recently moved from Lhasa to Beijing.

In prisons the Chinese built in my country Woeser's footnote cites Chapter 11 of Palden Gyatso's *Fire Under the Snow*.

by which one can distinguish words of forgiveness. Woeser is quoting the concluding words of stanza 9 in Czesław Miłosz's "With Trumpets and Zithers", first published as "Na trąbach i na cytrze" in *Miasto bez Imienia* (1969):

My dishonest memory did not preserve anything, save the triumph
of nameless births.

When I would hear a voice, it seemed to me I distinguished in it
words of forgiveness.

(Milosz 225)

Marked for death with two years' reprieve! The original is a two-
character abbreviation for a standard penalty in the PRC. At the end
of the two-year period of suspension, the prisoner is executed if he is
reported to have committed any crimes after his arrest. Otherwise
the sentence is commuted either to life imprisonment or, in the case
of good behavior, to a term of not less than fifteen years.

have fallen into evil hands. 蒙难, *mengnan.* Edifying stories about
revolutionary martyrs use this term to describe their capture.

They're both living buddhas. For reincarnate lamas, sometimes Woeser
uses a transliteration of the Tibetan word *trulku*; at other times, as
here, she uses the problematic but colloquial Chinese term 活佛
huofo.

Khampas from the East; that is, men of Kham. See Geographical
Note.

Bangri and Tenzin Delek Of Bangri, Woeser says in a footnote,
"Around 1997, he and his wife (Nyima Choedron) founded an
orphanage in Lhasa called the Gyatso Children's Home. They took
in 50 orphans who'd been begging in the streets. In 1999 they were
arrested on charges of espionage and activities endangering national
security, and were sentenced to 15 years and 10 years respectively.
The orphanage was forced to close, and many of the children, having
no other home, may have returned to the streets."

Bangri Chogtrul Rinpoche's troubles began on August 26, 1999,
when a building contractor was caught trying to raise the traditional
flag of Tibet in Potala Square. The man attempted to commit suicide
beneath the flagpole, but was apprehended and committed suicide
the following February while in detention. The evidence implicating
Bangri was that he had given the man money; but since the man had
been hired to repair the roof of the orphanage, this evidence seems

less than conclusive. Bangri is due to be released from prison in 2021. The International Campaign for Tibet has posted photographs of Bangri, Nyima Choedron, and the former Gyatso orphanage at http://www.savetibet.org/news/newsitem.php?id=920.

Tenzin Delek was a towering figure in Kham, a natural leader of his community. Woeser says of him in a footnote, "The humble Khampas around Nyagchu and Lithang are accustomed to call him 'The Big Lama.' He ranged among the farming villages and nomad pastures, preaching the scriptures and teaching the Dharma. He engaged in many charitable enterprises: founding schools for orphans, assisting the elderly who lived alone, repairing roads and bridges, protecting the environment, teaching the humble folk to give up smoking, drinking, gambling, and the taking of life. He was a living buddha who enjoyed the profound respect and love of the common people in those parts. But in December 2002, the authorities condemned him to death (with two years' reprieve) for the alleged crimes of 'incitement to split the nation' and 'plotting a series of bombings.' But this big case—which was handled in secrecy—was dubious in many respects. In the last two years the international community, the Tibetan exile community, and many intellectuals from inland China have all made vigorous appeals, demanding that the Chinese government abide by the law and re-open this case with a public trial. To date, these appeals have been ignored. Many local Tibetans were implicated in this case at the same time. One was a Tibetan named Lobsang Dondrup, who has already gone before the firing squad. Didi and other Tibetans have been sentenced to prison."

The dragnet was spread wide in the Tenzin Delek affair, as Human Rights Watch and other organizations have documented. Some of those arrested were accused of participating in the same alleged conspiracy; others, whose only apparent offense was to have sought legal counsel for Tenzin Delek, were detained on charges of convenience. I believe Woeser's reference to Didi (Chinese: *Da ti*) is to an in-law of Tenzin Delek, a businessman who made efforts to hire a lawyer from Beijing on Tenzin Delek's behalf and was detained for a few months on trumped-up charges.

exquisite mudras The placement of the hands in prescribed gestures is believed to aid meditation and strengthen the practitioner in the face of challenges. Mudras originated in Indian yoga and passed, with adaptations, into most schools of Buddhism. Zhu Zheqin was a Chinese popular musician who came to Lhasa to make a music video, "Yang Chenmo" (The Tibetan name of the Hindu goddess Saraswati, associated with learning and the arts). The video features close-ups of a monk's hands making mudras. That monk, Woeser explains in a footnote, was Bangri Rinpoche.

Who faced the government squarely and spoke out against the evils of the time After his arrest, Human Rights Watch published a detailed account of Tenzin Delek's life and work. He is remembered for speaking out in 1993 against local officials' theft of public land (for the sake of lucrative logging) in Nola township, and for founding unofficial schools and clinics in underserved areas. See *Trials of a Tibetan Monk: The Case of Tenzin Delek* at http://www.hrw.org/reports/2004/china0204/index.htm.

shouting the slogan all Tibetans know Probably *Bod Rangzen*, "Tibet Independence."

the PLA who were then fighting the Vietnamese. Seeking to "teach Vietnam a lesson," Deng Xiaoping sent 85,000 troops across the border without air support in February 1979. The Chinese withdrew less than a month later after the People's Liberation Army had advanced about 25 miles into Vietnam. Casualties were heavy and the results were ambiguous. This brief war may have strengthened Deng's hand at home; it discredited the Soviet Union, which failed to assist its Vietnamese ally; it revealed the need to modernize the PLA; it provided a pretext, if not a motive, for crushing the Democracy Wall movement in Beijing; and in Vietnam it inspired a persecution of ethnic Chinese with the result that many families fled abroad in a second wave of 'boat people.'

then took a bus alone out to Ganden Monastery Together with Sera and Drepung, Ganden was one (the oldest) of three major teaching monasteries in or near Lhasa. Founded early in the fifteenth century by Tsongkhapa, the charismatic scholar-saint whose birthplace is honored at Kumbum (Chinese *Ta'er*: see "A Mala that Was Meant to Be," p. 22), Ganden in its heyday was home to several thousand monks. It was greatly reduced in the 1950s. In the Cultural Revolution, it attracted the further attention of Red Guards with dynamite who left not one stone standing on another. The government has since rebuilt much of the site.

when he flung lungta from the mountaintop On going over a pass or reaching a summit, Tibetans are wont to cast to the winds a stack of small sheets of paper on which prayers have been written. The gesture can have a range of meanings and be associated with various emotions. *Lungta*, the name for the paper (or sometimes cloth), means "wind-horse." A sketch of a horse is often printed on it, in the center of the prayer.

The Party Secretary's comment For decades, the Communist Party exercised its control of society by placing a Party official known as the Party Secretary (党的书记, *dangde shuji*) inside every organization in China.   He, or sometimes she, enjoyed effectively unlimited disciplinary powers over both workers and management. State-owned enterprises still have this arrangement, but the private enterprises which in recent years have transformed the Chinese economy are mostly exempt.

Just what you'd expect from descendants of an ogress According to myth, the Tibetan people sprang from the union of a monkey bodhisattva (wise, gentle, compassionate) with an ogress of the rocks (lustful, selfish, obstinate). Tibetans invoke this ancestry to explain conflicting tendencies in their national character.

Yet in the Old Town's sweet-tea shops Woeser uses a Chinese term (转经路, *zhuanjinglu*) that can apply to any of three circumambulation paths in Lhasa: the Lingkor (outermost), the Barkor (the middle path, outside the Jokhang temple), and the Nangkor inside the temple complex. She could be referring here to either the Lingkor or the Barkor, and probably suggests the old part of town defined by them. She associates gossip with Lhasa's tea-shops in one of the essays included in *Notes on Tibet*, "A Killing Trip," of which an English translation can be found at http://www.tibetwrites.org.

"sugar-coated bullets" This awkward metaphor appears in official Chinese Communist pronouncements as early as 1955 and as late as 2004, but I am told it enjoyed particular currency during the Cultural Revolution. It denotes a corrupting or subversive attack disguised to seem attractive or benevolent. Such insidious enmity has most often been ascribed to the international bourgeoisie and the United States of America.

It's been said, "Tibetans' fear is palpable." The Chinese is not entirely clear. In her footnote, Woeser cites a Deutsche Welle broadcast from June 2002 that was based on an article in the May 30, 2002 issue of *Neue Zürcher Zeitung: "Angst im Schatten des Himalajas: In Tibet erstickt China jegliche Oppositionsregung."* The translation offered here relies on the original German: *Die Angst der Tibeter ist mit Händen zu greifen.*

the air has long been charged with fear Woeser may be saying that the fear is unconscious because all-pervading.

a reporter from Xinhua The Xinhua Press Agency is an organ of the State Council, that is, the central government of the PRC. Its website (http://www.xinhuanet.com) offers news not only in Chinese but also in several foreign languages including English. In October 2005, Reporters Without Borders (http://www.rsf.org) issued a scathing report, "The World's Biggest Propaganda Agency." Although frankly polemical, the report provides an interesting account of Xinhua's control by the Propaganda Department, drawn from interviews with present and former employees.

Sweet-scented lotus . . . Woeser has condensed the lyrics to one of the songs of the Drapchi Fourteen. In the liner notes to a CD published by the Free Tibet Campaign, *Seeing Nothing But the Sky: the Songs of Tibetan Nuns Recorded in a Chinese Prison,* the song is listed under the title "Committed Youths, Take an Oath for Independence."

Tears: A Final Song

This poem, notwithstanding its childlike rhythm and natural imagery, appears to be a political allegory, though I am not sure how specifically it should be applied. At the beginning of March the previous year, numerous protests (some violent) had broken out in Lhasa. Under martial law, things had quieted down quickly.

When an Iron Bird Flew Past Shédrak Mountain

my Teacher Literally, "my lama senior teacher" — a term equivalent to *guru*.

Mount Shédrak A rocky peak on the west side of the Yarlung valley, a region often described as the cradle of Tibetan civilization. The summit rises to 5500 meters; the cave which Woeser visited is at 4830 meters. Woeser writes Xizari (西杂日); the official Chinese rendering provided by the *Xizang Dimingzhi* is 西扎日, for which the pinyin would be xizhari. The traditional transliteration of the Tibetan name is Shel-brag, the simplified transliteration is Shédrak, and it is pronounced (approximately) 'shay-jack.' Although less than ten miles southwest of the small city of Tsethang, Shédrak is nestled in a rugged landscape without roads, and it takes several hours to reach the cave by a circuitous path. Dowman (191f.) describes the cave as a walled-in overhang about three meters deep and four meters wide at its opening, found near the base of a "phallic" peak. Sørensen and Hazod put the cave in the historical context of the early temple at Tradruk. They provide a satellite photograph (114) and a photograph of the cave sanctuary (134). The reader with access to Google Earth can view the landscape at coordinates 29°13' N   91°44' E.

the sublime Guru Rinpoche: An Indian mystic named Padmasambhava who came to Tibet in the eighth century C.E. and played a decisive part in the dissemination of Buddhism there.   Tibetans called him Guru Rinpoche, the precious master. In the tales of him that have been preserved, miraculous incidents are prominent. The classic medieval account of his life, which has come down in more than one form, purports to have been entrusted to his consort, the Dakini

Yeshe Tsogyal, and discovered hundreds of years later as one of the *terma* (hidden spiritual treasures) prized by the Nyingma school.

And the effulgence of his meditation lit up the mountain The original specifies a light "of many colors." In Tibetan iconography, this is not uncommon for great meditators, but Woeser may have been influenced by tales of *another* cave called Padma Shepuk, on the other side of the mountain and also associated with Guru Rinpoche. Sørensen and Hazod (264) describe a mandala centered on the Padma Shepuk, with "rays of light emanating from the lotus body of Padmasambhava while he meditates in the grotto. They flow in different colours in the five directions...."

a silver aircraft—no, an iron bird The image of an iron bird echoes a prophecy attributed to Guru Rinpoche:

> When the iron bird flies and horses run on wheels, the Tibetan people will be scattered like ants and the Dharma will come to the land of the red men.

This prophecy, often cited but never sourced, may have originated in the twentieth century as a *vaticinium ex eventu*. The first person to inform the translator of a documented pre-modern source will be credited in any later editions.

Mt. Shédrak had been the embodiment of a demon I have been unable to find this tale attested elsewhere. It resembles the mythical geography of the Lhasa area according to which temples were constructed in certain places in order to pin down and render helpless a primordial demon who dwelt there (Barnett 55). Such imagery expresses Buddhism's triumph over the indigenous religions of Tibet.

Strange Light

Strange Light The poet lends the dazzling high-altitude daylight of Tibet a symbolism that is by no means positive. It represents a harsh reality which (like ultraviolet light) does harm, imperceptibly, to living things. In a personal communication, she explained that the indefinite "someone" in line 14 (translated "a Higher Power") who devised this light "represents a kind of overbearing power, above and beneath and all around ... Perhaps it's a Creator God; perhaps it is some political regime, but in any case it is in control and it is utterly despotic." When she wonders whether it is possible to attain the "place of shadow," she is expressing a desire, still ambivalent, to find refuge in religion.

with great expectations The original is 心比天高, half of a phrase applied to a star-crossed young woman in the eighteenth-century classic *Dream of the Red Chamber*: "The heart reaches high [but one's fate is bleak]."

the palace of the past "The Potala," Woeser explained in a personal communication, "but not as it exists today."

Tsangyang Gyatso See notes to "Tsangyang Gyatso" on pp. 103-4. The Fifth Dalai Lama began construction of the Potala. The Regent of the Lhasa government concealed his death for many years (and had the successor, Tsangyang Gyatso, selected and trained in secret) to ensure that the great work would be completed. The "perhaps" attached to the mention of the age at which the Sixth Dalai Lama died is a nod towards an alternative history according to which he escaped his captors near Lake Kokonor and lived for forty more years as a wandering holy man. This version of history was probably inspired by the career of an impersonator of the Sixth Dalai Lama (Aris 170).

A Quick Note in the Small Hours

The Sandman The original is "my sleep-inducing insect," a traditional term slightly less fanciful than the European Sandman, but with the same figurative sense.

a tsongpa hustling nine-eyed beads The Tibetan word *tsongpa* denotes an enterprising businessman, with (depending on the context) a suggestion of sharp practice. Nine-eyed Dzi beads are prized as amulets: for details, see the note on p. 118.

even livelier than One Hundred Years of Solitude The writings of Gabriel García Márquez have been both popular and influential in China.

New Shöl Village (Chinese 雪新村 *xuexincun*, Tibetan *Shöl Drongsar*.) A neighborhood behind the Potala, named after the old village of Shöl in front of the Potala that was dismantled as part of a modernization program.

"May Heaven protect the well-fed masses" A satirical song composed by the folk-rock musician Zhang Chu.

The Blessed One The reference is to one or more bodhisattvas, figures who function as Saviors in Mahayana Buddhism.

Dreamshadow

Did we meet, he and I? This poem was inspired by a journey to eastern Tibet in which the poet met a *trulku*, an incarnate lama, who had suffered during the Cultural Revolution and whose story moved her so deeply she felt there must be some bond between them, perhaps from a previous life.

on what rusting vajra bell? The vajra and bell are ritual implements used together in many of the ceremonies of Tibetan Buddhism. The vajra, a pronged metallic scepter, is variously interpreted as a diamond or a thunderbolt. The vajra and bell represent masculine and feminine principles respectively. Sometimes the two are combined in a single artifact, a bell with a vajra-shaped handle: that seems to be what is referred to here.

For days, now, I am partnered with a fine steed Her journey continued into the grasslands of Kham. She encountered a handsome young man, the strawberries, the fish, and the rainbow as she passed through the sparsely populated landscape, still reflecting on her encounter with the lama.

After a Few Years

You're where we started / I'm at the other end   The literal geography behind these phrases is an imaginary line from Chengdu, where the poet had graduated from college in 1988, to Lhasa, where she had recently moved after a couple of years in Kangding. The "you" is a young man whom the poet had known when they were both students in Chengdu.

With a scarred face   The phrase in Chinese suggests brutal violence. The poet has explained she intends it as a metaphor for sexual experience.

I want to speak but hold my peace. / You want to speak but hold your peace   An allusion to a Song Dynasty poem by Xin Qiji (1140-1207 C.E.), "Written on a wall by the path to Mt. Bo."

Return to Lhasa

in Tibetan style (no glazed tiles!)   After Deng Xiaoping began the marketization of the Chinese economy in 1992, a great deal of investment began flowing into Lhasa from inland provinces. Initially it took the form of drab construction. Of the architecture of this period, Barnett writes, "The new buildings had, at least along more important streets, one aesthetic embellishment: the concrete frontages were usually clad with large white tiles that for Western visitors made the streets look like the interior of a giant toilet or bathroom" (88).

You unna-stand?   The original is an ungrammatical phrase (*ni di mingbai*, 你的明白) used by imperious Japanese villains in Chinese films of a certain era.

fake palm trees   Presumably miniature souvenirs. For the plastic palm trees that were installed to adorn Yuthok Lam, see Barnett 103.

the celebrated Qinghai-Tibet railway   In August 2006, Woeser published an essay about the new rail link in Hong Kong's *Open* magazine. It appeared in translation as "The Iron Dragon Has Come" in *China Rights Forum,* No. 4, 2006 (pp. 19-22).

for a glimpse of Lhasa's new look Echoing the refrain from a 1959 propaganda song "Strolling Around the New City" (逛新城).

at the corner of New Shöl Village See note on p. 115. Here the reference may be to a street of the same name which marks the eastern edge of Shöl Drongsar.

A Ganzi Gang and a Suining Gang These underworld organizations are named after prefectures in Sichuan Province from which, presumably, their members come.

the Red Supermarket This store has since been torn down and replaced by a larger supermarket. The map on p. 132 indicates its location.

I offered her a yuan Pilgrims performing prostrations at sacred sites have often travelled far. It is considered meritorious to support them. There is no suggestion of mendicancy.

That's become the vogue in Lhasa, to sew otter or leopard fur onto your winter coat. Two months after this poem was written, the Dalai Lama urged Tibetans to stop wearing fur. His aim was to slow the extinction of rare species on the Tibetan Plateau and also to encourage stricter observance of the Buddhist prohibition against killing. There was a strong popular response in which large quantities of fur were publicly burned all over the Tibetan cultural region. Since then, the authorities of the PRC have required musicians, dancers, television presenters, and others to wear fur as a condition of public performance in Tibet.

The word translated "coat" is literally "Tibetan robe," a reference to the ankle-length outer garment called the *chuba.* It is usually made of sheepskin and closed with a sash.

...cottage industries in Linxia, Gansu. Linxia is an ancient Muslim (Hui minority) trading center in Gansu Province.

And take common stones for Dzi beads Dzi beads are cylindrical stones of chalcedony (a form of quartz whose crystalline structure is not visible to the eye: agate and carnelian are the best-known varieties) that experts say have been painted with metal salts or other chemicals before being fired in a kiln. This treatment etches a two-tone pattern conventionally consisting of either jagged lines or circles called "eyes." Tradition ascribes medicinal powers to Dzi beads, which are usually drilled so they can be hung on a necklace, and the most sought-after are those with nine "eyes." Though similar artifacts can be traced to India and the Ancient Near East, the term Dzi denotes a distinctively Tibetan product. Its Chinese name, "Sky gem," reflects the legend that the beads fall to earth when discarded by heavenly beings. They are prized when believed to be antique.

the deep-red Tsuklakhang The Tsuklakhang is the Tibetan name for the complex in Lhasa that includes the Jokhang Temple. Its oldest elements date from the seventh century C.E. The word for "deep red" is one Woeser often uses for the maroon color of monks' robes. In addition to describing the temple façade at sunset, therefore, the word here probably suggests the ingrained Buddhist character of Tibet.

And I behold Jowo Rinpoche again   A gilded copper image of the twelve-year-old Buddha Shakyamuni, traditionally believed to have been donated as part of the dowry of the Chinese Princess Wencheng in the seventh century. " . . . the image is also called 'the great liberation through seeing' (Tib.: *mthong grol chen mo*) because merit is believed to be accumulated merely by seeing the Jo[w]o" (von Schroeder 926).

Tradition has it there's a lake beneath the temple The Tsuklakhang "was certainly built on marshy wetlands if not a lake" (Alexander 31).

Showers of 1990

Showers of 1990   In the world in which the speaker finds herself, rain defiles, and humanity unknowingly consorts with demons and relishes spiritual poison. Through literature she seeks an ideal world.

This sets her apart and exposes her to criticism. Many of her terms suggest an ambivalence; she is not yet sure of her choices. 1990 was the year Woeser returned to her birthplace, Lhasa, after growing up in Kham and attending college in the capital of Sichuan Province. Written a year later, this poem takes stock of the move.

I wash my hands when it thunders   An involuntary expression of anxiety, but it also fits the poem's symbolic scheme.

And never guess the enormous secret   In a personal communication, Woeser identified the secret: that what worldly people drink so merrily is the "five poisons." Buddhist literature offers more than one enumeration of them—Woeser mentioned Greed, Anger, Ignorance, Egoism, and Envy.

Escapist inconsistency   Literally, "a small movement [or action] that can find a hideout somewhere." 'Small movement' (小动作) was a cant term at the time of the Cultural Revolution for minor, private failures to live up to a publicly-avowed socialist morality. The milder sort of self-criticism session would focus on these lapses. Woeser is describing the search for a private space in her own life, one that would sustain values incompatible with the public order of things. It required often hiding her true feelings and thus imposed a strain.

How many showers must this body of Now   Referring to the "other rain" (translated "the rains of Heaven") that she associates with poetic inspiration.

before it bears fruit quickly   Literally, "Morning flowers gathered at dusk." The productivity she has in mind may be of a literary nature, because this phrase was the title of a collection of autobiographical essays by the celebrated writer Lu Xun (1881– 1936).

Singing as best I can, or forgetting   In the refrain to another poem not included in this volume ("Another Embodiment"), Woeser juxtaposes artistic expression and forgetfulness. What she means depends on what would be forgotten. If it is worldly distractions, then the forgetting enables the singing. If it is the subject of her song, then she sings so as not to forget.

You Must Remember This

This dialogue would seem to occur between a Chinese man and a Tibetan woman who have met in Lhasa. She corrects him when he uses the Chinese name for the street that rings the Jokhang Temple and again, more subtly, when he focuses on their individual selves instead of the mysterious fate that has brought them together. That important relationships are never accidental but flow from a destiny that defies analysis is a belief which Tibetans and Chinese share.

You hear low voices of entreaty Along with pilgrims circumambulating the temple and merchants offering their wares, there are usually beggars present in the Barkor.

Parents

a youth at ease with weapons Woeser's father, Tsering Dorje, was the son of a Tibetan woman and a Chinese man who had come west during the turbulent 1930s. Tsering Dorje was only thirteen years old when the PLA swept through Kham, but with his father's encouragement he joined the army and eventually rose to become the deputy commander of the Lhasa military region.

Two rivers joined It may be only a coincidence that the name of Chamdo, a Khampa town where the PLA decisively defeated the Tibetan Army in 1950, means "Two Rivers."

Roaming the Infinite Night

In three sections, the poem (written soon after Woeser graduated from college) describes three kinds of spiritual darkness: 1) the ignorance and distorted judgment of a generation victimized by a deceptive education; 2) the cynicism of an intellectually corrupt class of teachers and leaders who foist such education upon the young; 3) the sufferings of those who, because they are receptive to truth and bear witness to it, lose their ability to function in a harsh and deceitful world. The latter injury the poet describes as a blindness, and she connects it in her imagination to the blindness of Homer.

the eye of burning gold The first chapters of the Ming Dynasty classic *Journey to the West* recount the prior adventures of the Monkey King. After causing trouble in Heaven and defying efforts to execute him, the Monkey King was cast into a furnace. The fire did not kill him, however; it gave him a burning, golden eye that could see through disguises and deceptions.

We have long since handed that back to You Today Woeser identifies the "You" of this poem as the Buddhas or Bodhisattvas who have attained enlightenment and omniscience, and who offer mankind a way to Truth. At the time of composition she may have had a less specific understanding of ultimate reality. She had recorded in some college poems a curiosity about religion in general, but it was a couple of years before she began feeling drawn to Buddhism. The "different kind of speech" mentioned in this line is Truth, considered the gift of a transcendent power which granted it to the human world but left it vulnerable, like an 'abandoned baby.' Responding to that gift with integrity requires following the gift's path back to its source, the "path to Heaven." Content with or paralyzed by a world of falsehoods, most people have refused (handed back) the gift of truth and have lost touch with it.

But we can't stop feeding vermin. The "vermin" are innate flaws of character.

I yearn to go blind utterly Thubten Yeshe writes, "Tibetan lamas often say, 'Not seeing is the perfect seeing'" (69).

Nightfall on June 2nd

On top, the crouching deer are lifelike The statuary of a pair of deer bracketing a wheel is typically found over the main gate of a Buddhist temple. The image alludes to the Buddha's first sermon in Deer Park at Benares, at which he is said to have started the wheel of the Dharma turning.

The Illness of Tibet

four-and-eighty thousand Buddhist literature abounds in hyperbolical enumerations. The poem is alluding to three strands of traditional thought.

One stems from the belief that the Pali Canon, the Scripture of the Theravada branch of Buddhism, contains 84,000 chapters or discrete teachings. The *locus classicus* is verses 1023-1024 of the Theragāthā, in which the disciple Ananda says after the Buddha's death:

> *This Gotama stands on the way leading to quenching, on which the teachings of the Buddha, kinsman of the sun, are well-founded. 82,000 I received from the Buddha, 2,000 from the bhikkhus. These 84,000 are current teachings.*
> (Elders' Verses 94)

Although the canon of Tibetan Buddhism (the Kangyur) differs substantially from that of the Theravadins, Tibetan Buddhists claim that theirs, too, contains 84,000 teachings. The same number is predicated of the "afflictive emotions" (the whole spectrum of "mental poisons" comprising various forms of desire, hatred, ignorance, and combinations thereof) in order to say that each teaching is the remedy for one afflictive emotion.

The second strand of thought results from substituting the term "Dharma door" (in Chinese, 法门) in the assertion that there are 84,000 teachings. In popular usage, a Dharma door is an approach to Buddhist belief and practice, one that will be suitable for some individuals but not for others. Buddhism prides itself on its acceptance of a diversity of approaches to enlightenment. That there are 84,000 Dharma doors means that there are many approaches to the truth, and that individuals of different dispositions and needs can find forms of practice and conceptualization that are suited to them.

The third strand is the vegetative metaphor. Here it suggests Tibetan medicine's penchant for herbs and other plants with healing properties. The metaphor concretizes the idea that the teachings offer a remedy for afflictive emotions. But it also echoes the fifth chapter of the Lotus Sutra, where vegetation of different sizes symbolizes people of different capacities and the rain represents the teaching of the Dharma, which each person absorbs according to his nature and ability.

Come Home

The eagle of my spirit Literally, 'my divine eagle.' I am unsure of the exact sense. Clearly it has heroic overtones. The term appears in a song composed by Tashi Dawa and popularized by Yadong in 1996, "Yearning for the Divine Eagle" (向往神鹰), but there it refers to an airplane. Woeser's choice of a noble bird to symbolize the Dalai Lama evokes the memory of Tsangyang Gyatso's most celebrated verse, usually read as a prophecy of his reincarnation:

> *White crane!*
> *Lend me your wings.*
> *I won't go far, only to Lithang,*
> *And then I'll come back.*

I am obliged to Yangdon Dhondup for pointing out these connections in a personal communication. For an interpretative overview of modern Tibetan popular music, see her article ("Dancing").

Om mani peme hung: A Tibetan rendering of the Sanskrit mantra "Om mani padme hum." A mantra is a short, sonorous phrase repeated in order to express prayer, focus meditation, or avert misfortune. Inherited and elaborated from the Hindu scriptures of the second millennium BCE, mantras play a vital role in Tibetan Buddhism. The original meaning of this mantra is disputed (many scholars demur at the popular interpretation *'the jewel is in the lotus')*. It is certain, however, that it long ago became an invocation of the bodhisattva Avalokiteshvara (Tibetan: Chenrezig), the embodiment of compassion, of whom the Dalai Lama is believed to be an emanation. It would be difficult to overstate its ubiquity in traditional Tibetan life: carved on *mani* stones, it greets the traveler in the wilderness; inscribed on cylinders (*mani* wheels), it is counted as uttered whenever they are spun; and it forms a murmured undertone in the life of the devout.

March 10   On March 10, 1959, a huge crowd surrounded the Norbulingka, summer residence of the Dalai Lama, who was then twenty-three years old, in an effort to frustrate what were perceived as preparations by the PLA to kidnap or kill him. A week later, after the PLA had brought artillery to the outskirts of Lhasa and opened fire on his residence, the Dalai Lama escaped by night and made his way to India (Avedon 50-56). "A Vow" (p. 33) is likewise dated March 10 and alludes to the same events.

Positioning

Woeser recalls that at the time of writing she was trying to put Tibet and its culture out of her mind.

Of Mixed Race

She's but the shadow of a dream whose tints have faded "Shadow of a dream" evokes the notion, common to Buddhism and some strands of Taoism, that what we take to be our real life is only a fragment of a fantasy. "Whose tints have faded" has a positive meaning: the "tints" are adventitious or deceptive elements. As they fade, a person or thing comes to be seen in a truer light.

The Past

Many a lotus, eight petals blooming The open lotus may represent the land itself surrounding the mountains, or perhaps the religious culture which dotted the landscape with shrines and prayer flags. The specification of eight petals may simply suggest perfection and beauty. Traditional iconography employed the lotus as a throne for a deity, with as few as four or as many as one thousand petals. There was also an implied connection with the system of yogic *chakras* (energy nodes within the human body), which are conventionally represented as lotuses. In that system the heart *chakra* is an eight-petaled lotus, and therefore the eight-petaled lotus often serves as the throne of Chenrezig, emanation of compassion. But as Beer notes, "the complexity of Vajrayana imagery rarely accommodates rules of generality" (38).

Yunnan, in sight of Mt. Khawa Karpo In a footnote, Woeser says the first two lines came to her as she watched the sun set behind Mt. Khawa Karpo (Chinese: Kawagebo), while she was in Yunnan visiting a Tibetan district that is being marketed to tourists under the name of "Shangri-la."

GEOGRAPHICAL NOTE

The intricate geography, earth science, and political history of the Tibetan Plateau are beyond the scope of this book. This note aims merely to make the place names in Woeser's poems intelligible to all readers.

History has given Tibet more than one gazetteer. Most of the places about which Woeser writes have both a Chinese name and a Tibetan name. (In the northeast, there are Mongolian names as well.) In some cases, the Chinese name is a transliteration (not always close) of the Tibetan; in others, it is unrelated. Even before the 1950 invasion, the eastern parts of the country saw a complicated ebb and flow of influence and settlement. Pre-modern Tibet had a relaxed attitude about defining boundaries. (See McGranahan 268 and her account of the Simla conference (269-74) that sought to clarify Tibet's borders before the First World War.)

Because Woeser's story involves the respectful rediscovery of Tibetan traditions, I have preferred for this translation the Tibetan forms of place names. I do not mean to disparage the Chinese nomenclature: that would be silly, though the rebranding of Gyeltang as Shangri-la is a special case that invites derision. Dartsedo I have called by its Chinese name, Kangding, because it figures here only as a place where Woeser lived, and when she lived there she was mostly in the orbit of Chinese culture.

The ambiguities do not end with the choice of names. Tibetans refer often to the regions of Amdo, Kham, and Ü-Tsang, which the reader will not find in any atlas. These are sometimes glossed as the provinces of old Tibet, but that term implies a more precise and official division than the country ever knew. Of these traditional zones, there were more than three. Ü-

Tsang is the amalgamation of what were once two distinct districts Ü and Tsang, with power centers at Lhasa and Shigatse, respectively. In the far west, the region of Ngari (especially the ancient kingdom of Guge at its southern end[*]) played a crucial role in the transmission of Buddhism during the eleventh century C.E., but later waned. To the northwest stretches the vast, high-altitude prairie called the Changtang (or Jangtang). It is more extensive than the nature preserve which bears its name today.

It is vital to grasp the locations of Kham and Amdo, because down to the present day differences in dialect, garb, and customs have given these areas a distinct character. Unfortunately, the provincial boundaries drawn by the PRC (demarcating the Tibet Autonomous Region, Qinghai, Gansu, Sichuan, and Yunnan) appear calculated to fragment these regions and dilute any sense of identity they may have enjoyed.

Using the fine resources offered online by the Tibetan & Himalayan Digital Library (http://www.thdl.org), I have sketched some maps on the following pages. Their limitations are apparent at a glance. I trust no reader will rely on them to navigate the Changtang, or plot an approach to Kailash, or judge a Sino-Indian boundary dispute.

The first map shows the traditional zones of Tibet superimposed on the provincial boundaries of this part of the PRC. The second, spread across two pages, shows the approximate locations of places mentioned in the text. The last sketch is of central Lhasa, showing the relative location of landmarks and streets that are mentioned in the text. It is based, in part, on a tracing of a Lhasa City map published by the Centre for Occupied Tibet Studies, Amnye Machen Institute.

---

[*] The author photo on the back of this book's dust jacket was taken at the ruins of the palace of Guge.

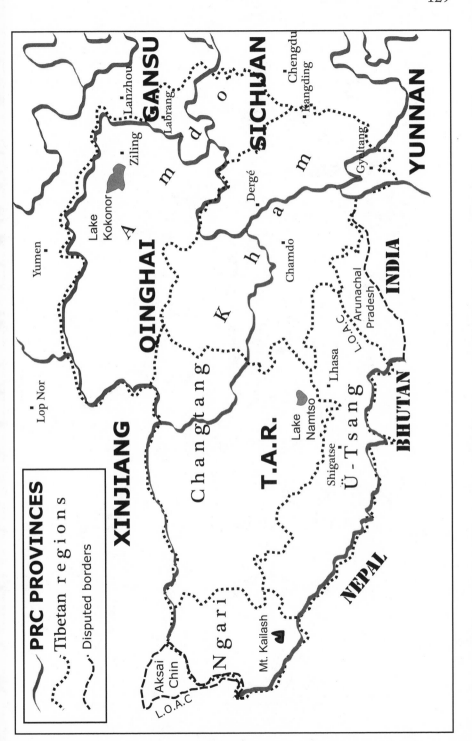

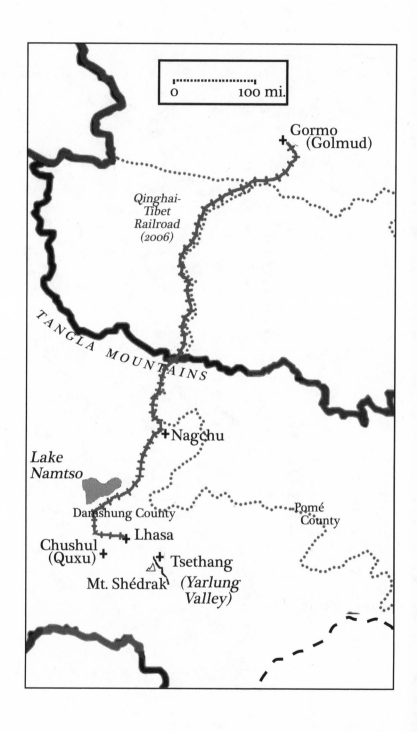

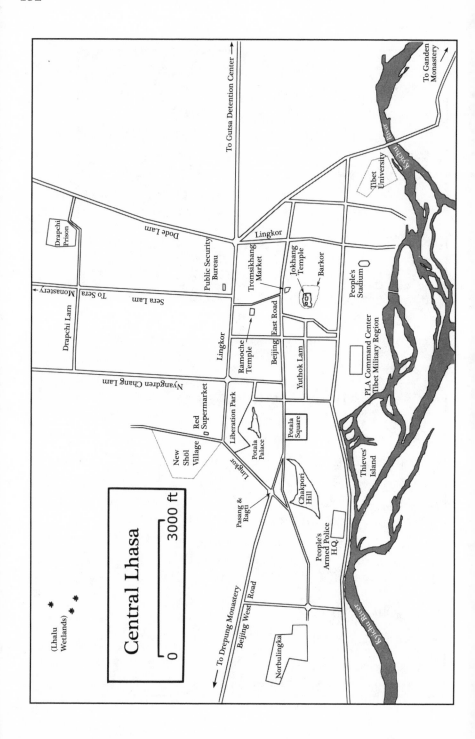

Central Lhasa

0 — 3000 ft

REFERENCES

Alexander, André. *The Temples of Lhasa: Tibetan Buddhist Architecture from the 7th to the 21st centuries*. Chicago: Serindia Publications, 2005.

Aris, Michael. *Hidden Treasures and Secret Lives: A Study of Pemalingpa (1450-1521) and the Sixth Dalai Lama (1683-1706)*. London and New York: Kegan Paul International, 1989.

Avedon, John F. *In Exile from the Land of Snows*. New York: HarperCollins, 1997. (first ed. 1984, Knopf)

Barnett, Robert (ed.). *A Poisoned Arrow: The Secret Petition of the 10th Panchen Lama*. London: Tibet Information Network, 1998.

Barnett, Robert. *Lhasa: Streets with Memories*. New York: Columbia University Press, 2006.

---. "Thunder from Tibet." *The New York Review of Books*. 55/9: May 29, 2008.

Beer, Robert. *The Encyclopedia of Tibetan Symbols and Motifs*. Chicago: Serindia Publications, 2004.

Chang, Garma C. C. *The Hundred Thousand Songs of Milarepa*. Boston: Shambhala, 1999.

Chang, Jung. *Wild Swans: Three Daughters of China*. London: Flamingo, 1991. (re-issued several times in several countries)

Chen Jo-Hsi. *The Execution of Mayor Yin and Other Stories from the Great Proletarian Cultural Revolution*. Bloomington: Indiana University Press, 1978.

Dowman, Keith. *The Power-Places of Central Tibet: The Pilgrim's Guide*. London and New York: Routledge & Kegan Paul, 1988.

The Elders' Verses I: Theragāthā. Trans. K. R. Norman. (Pali Text Society Translation Series No. 38). London: Luzac and Company, Ltd., 1969.

Eliot, T. S. *Collected Poems 1909 – 1962*. New York: Harcourt, Brace & World, 1970.

French, Patrick. *Tibet, Tibet: a Personal History of a Lost Land*. New York: Random House, 2003.

Ginsberg, Allen. *Selected Poems 1947 – 1995*. New York: HarperCollins, 1996.

Goldstein, Melvyn C., Dawei Sherap, and William R. Siebenschuh. *A Tibetan Revolutionary: The Political Life and Times of Bapa Phüntso Wangye*. Berkeley and Los Angeles: University of California Press, 2004.

Gyurme Dorje. *Footprint Tibet Handbook* (2nd ed.). Bath: Footprint Handbooks, 1999.

MacFarquhar, Roderick, and Michael Schoenhals. *Mao's Last Revolution*. Cambridge: Harvard University Press, 2006.

McGranahan, Carole. "Empire and the status of Tibet: British, Chinese, and Tibetan negotiations, 1913-1934." *The History of Tibet*. Ed. Alex McKay. London: Routledge, 2003. 267-295.

Milosz, Czeslaw. *New and Collected Poems: 1931-2001*. New York: HarperCollins, 2001.

Moneyhon, Matthew. "Controlling Xinjiang: Autonomy on China's 'New Frontier'." *Asian-Pacific Law & Policy Journal 3/1 (Winter 2002)*. 120-152.

Mulvenon, James C., and Andrew N.D. Yang. *The People's Liberation Army as Organization, Reference vol. 1*. Santa Monica: RAND, 2002.

Palden Gyatso. *Fire Under the Snow*. Trans. Tsering Shakya. London: Harville Press, 1997. United States edition published by Grove Press as *The Autobiography of a Tibetan Monk*.

Powers, John. *Introduction to Tibetan Buddhism*. Ithaca: Snow Lion Publications, 1995.

Ricard, Matthieu. *Tibet: an Inner Journey*. New York: Thames & Hudson, 2006.

Schroeder, Ulrich von. *Buddhist Sculptures in Tibet*. Hong Kong: Visual Dharma Publications, 2001.

Shakya, Tsering. "Blood in the Snows: Reply to Wang Lixiong." *New Left Review*, May-June 2002, 15:39-60.

---. *The Dragon in the Land of Snows: A History of Modern Tibet Since 1947*. London and New York: Penguin, 1999.

Simmer-Brown, Judith. *Dakini's Warm Breath: The Feminine Principle in Tibetan Buddhism*. Boston: Shambhala, 2001.

Sørensen, Per K. *Divinity Secularized: an enquiry into the nature and form of the songs ascribed to the Sixth Dalai Lama*. Vienna: Wiener Studien zur Tibetologie und Buddhismuskunde, 1990.

---, and Guntram Hazod. *Thundering Falcon: An Inquiry into the History and Cult of Khra-'brug, Tibet's First Buddhist Temple*. Vienna: Verlag der Österreichischen Akademie der Wissenschaften, 2005.

Wang Lixiong. "Reflections on Tibet." *New Left Review*, March-April 2002, 14:79-111.

Wei Se. *Forbidden Memory: Tibet During the Cultural Revolution* [Chinese title: 杀劫]. Taipei: Locus Publishing, 2006.

Yangdon Dhondup. "Dancing to the Beat of Modernity: the Rise and Development of Tibetan Pop Music." *Tibetan Modernities: Notes*

from the Field on Social and Cultural Change. Eds.
Robert Barnett and Ronald Schwartz. Leiden: Brill,
2008.

---. "Roar of the Snow Lion: Tibetan Poetry in Chinese."
Modern Tibetan Literature and Social Change. Eds.
Lauran Hartley and Patricia Schiaffini-Vedani.
Durham: Duke University Press, 2008. 32-60.

Yeshe, Thubten. *Introduction to Tantra: The Transformation of
Desire.* Somerville MA: Wisdom Publications, 2001
(first ed. 1987).

Yeshe Tsogyal. *The Lotus-Born: the Life Story of
Padmasambhava.* Trans. Eric Pema Kunsang. Boston:
Shambhala, 1993.

COLOPHON

This book was set in the typeface designed by the eighteenth-century gunsmith and type founder William Caslon and adapted for the digital age by Adobe Systems Incorporated.

A protean talent can persist through generations. The translator received his first lessons in Latin grammar forty years ago from Denis Caslon—scholar, impresario, and direct descendant of the type founder.

BONAE LITTERAE REDDUNT HOMINES

Copies of this book can be ordered online:

http://www.RaggedBanner.com